Advanced Legal Writing Workshop

Advanced Legal Writing Workshop

By Wayne Schiess

Other books by Wayne Schiess:

- *Legal Writing Nerd: Be One*
- *Plain Legal Writing: Do It*
- *Fine Points for Legal Writing*
- *Writing for the Legal Audience*

For Sarah, Cory, Anna, Davis, Noah, and Logan.

Table of Contents

Advanced Legal Writing Workshop

Preface

This book was written and designed for a course I teach at the University of Texas School of Law called Advanced Legal Writing Workshop. The course is meant (and the book is, too) to help law students master roughly 50 advanced concepts, techniques, and mechanics of legal writing.

Why study advanced topics? Because lawyers are professional writers. Because having a high writing IQ (that is, knowing a lot of stuff about writing and what that stuff is called) correlates with overall strong writing ability. And because studying advanced topics and mastering as many as you can will make all your legal-writing activities go better: generating ideas and arguments, outlining, composing, and most important—editing.

So set a goal to master these advanced topics and make them part of your writing radar. Your writing radar is what tingles when you encounter a writing problem: you don't know every technique or rule, but you know when something's not right. You know when you don't really know. And you know when you need to look it up. Soon these advanced topics will be become second nature.

Good luck.

I express my gratitude to *Austin Lawyer* magazine for allowing me to write about so many legal topics for so many years, to the University of

Texas School of Law for allowing me to teach the course, and to the students for indulging my unconventional teaching style.

Wayne Schiess
August 2019

P.S. Some quotations in this book have been cleaned up.

Introduction

What I Wish I'd Known about Legal Writing

Here are four things I wish I'd known about legal writing before I became a lawyer.

I wish I'd known
... that law was a writing profession.

I went to law school thinking law was an oral profession, but lawyers mostly write. A lot. In a recent survey of lawyers in Washington D.C., nearly 70% said they spend half their time writing, and many said they spend 75%. [1]Lawyers are professional writers, paid to produce quality written work, and lots of it. I wish I'd known that.

... that becoming a good legal writer would take years.

I thought I was a good writer in college, and I thought the basic training I received in law school would enable me to write well in practice. I was wrong.

---

1 Catherine H. Finn & Claudia Diamond, *Are We Listening?*, Washington Lawyer (Jan. 2015).

Malcolm Gladwell's *Outliers* reports on a theory of developing expertise, suggesting that it takes 10,000 hours to develop expertise in a particular area. If the theory is right, it applies to legal writing. So if you work 2000 hours a year, and 1000 are spent writing, it'll take you 10 years to become an expert legal writer. That's a long time.

But it's not enough to just write for 10,000 hours. You need to work at it: study, learn, and implement what you've learned. If you don't study your craft—if you just write on auto-pilot—it'll take you more than 10,000 hours. So work at it and hang in there. Accept critique and learn from it. But be patient—with yourself and with others—because mastering legal writing takes time. I wish I'd known that.

... that time pressure impedes good writing.

Law is a busy, demanding profession. Many lawyers feel compelled or are compelled to take on more work than is ideal. Deadlines loom, and the day has only 24 hours. The heavy workload and deadlines often impede effective legal writing.

Let's take editing as an example. If your writing is mediocre, maybe it's because you don't know how to edit; maybe you know how, but you're too lazy. Both possible, both unlikely.

If you don't edit well, it's probably because you don't have time. Yet editing is what makes mediocre writing good and good writing great. Too often, in a busy law practice, careful editing gets sacrificed. There's no easy solution to the time crunch, but here are some ideas:

- start the draft sooner
- finish the draft sooner
- adopt deadlines for the draft and the first edit
- raise your writing IQ so your drafts are stronger and need less editing
- work late, eat the time, sacrifice your personal life

I told you it isn't easy.

... about the best sources on legal writing.

I didn't own a book on legal writing until I quit practicing law and began teaching legal writing. How could that be? If I'd studied journalism, I would've owned books on writing. Likewise if I'd studied English composition. But I finished law school and entered a writing profession owning not a single source on legal writing.

Given what was available when I graduated from law school in 1989, I wish I'd had these sources:

- The Texas Law Review *Manual on Usage and Style* (today you'll want the 14th edition)
- *A Dictionary of Modern Legal Usage*, by Bryan A. Garner (now *Garner's Dictionary of Legal Usage*, 3rd)
- *How To Write Plain English*, by Rudolf Flesch (still available from used booksellers)

Ultimately, I wish I'd taken the skill of legal writing more seriously. Lawyers young and old—you're warned.

Lawyers As Professional Writers

For three reasons, you, as a lawyer, are a professional writer.

Lawyers are paid to write. That takes you out of amateur status. And most of us don't write a little; we write a lot. I remember when I began working at a law firm that I was surprised at how much writing there was. "Gosh," I thought. "Why didn't anyone tell me I was going to be doing so much writing?" If writing is a significant part of your job, you're a professional writer.

Lawyers' writing deals with complex topics and affects rights, money, and liberty. Usually, there's a lot riding on your writing: your client's money, your client's rights and, in the criminal setting, your client's liberty or even life. If writing with that kind of pressure weren't enough, there's the complexity of the subject matter. The law is complicated, and writing about complex topics with a lot at stake is demanding work. Grasping the complex subject matter and writing about it clearly are the hallmarks of a professional writer.

Lawyers' written work is subject to serious scrutiny. Legal writing gets scrutinized and criticized and satirized. Your legal documents can end up in front of multiple audiences, and each has a chance to evaluate your writing. Your supervisor, who can hire and fire, promote and demote, gets to inspect your writing. Opposing counsel gets paid to find your mistakes—sort of a professional writing critic. Your client, the one paying you to write, can examine your writing, of course. And in litigation the judge is, well, judging it. Writing facing that much scrutiny is professional writing.

Convinced? I hope so. If not, go read *The Lawyer's Guide to Writing Well*, by Goldstein and Lieberman. It convinced me that lawyers are professional writers. Once you're convinced, take some steps to act like a professional writer. That idea is a theme of *The Lawyer's Guide to Writing Well*: lawyers are professional writers, and we should act like it.

Here are some ways.

Professional writers consult writing references, and lawyers should, too. The sources I recommend are listed in various places in this book and in a comprehensive list at the end. Once you've started using a writing reference, try to get others to do it. Having a reliable and consistent source for answering writing questions will raise the writing IQ of everyone in your office.

Professional writers continue to learn. For lawyers, that could mean attending a legal-writing CLE. Better yet, you could volunteer to present a legal-writing CLE. A great way to improve your writing knowledge is to write a paper about legal writing and then teach a class about it. Continuing to learn could also mean reading books about writing. Here are two gems: *On Writing Well* by William Zinsser and *Legal Writing: Sense and Nonsense* by David Mellinkoff.

Professional writers use editors, and lawyers need them too. You have several options, from more expensive to less expensive. You could hire an in-house editor or writing specialist (expensive). You could have every lawyer in the office attend training on copy editing (moderate). Or you could ask a trusted colleague to edit your writing (cheap—for you).

Whatever you do, remember what professional writers know: bad writing becomes good and good writing becomes great only by editing.

Here's one more idea: start a writing group. Select or invite a group of lawyers to meet over lunch once a week to discuss good writing. Have everyone take a turn offering a document for the group to read in advance and then discuss at the meeting. You'll get two benefits: the writing IQ of everyone in the group is bound to rise, and you'll learn that accepting constructive feedback is a great way to improve your writing.

And improving is part of being a professional writer.

Improving Your Writing Throughout Your Career

Let me offer advice for a career-long pursuit of excellence in legal writing. I'll start with a question:

- Are the legal writing classes you had in law school the last writing training you'll need?

If you practice bankruptcy law, was a law-school course the last bankruptcy training you'll need? I know the answer to that because I was a bankruptcy lawyer before I became a legal-writing teacher. The answer is no. You'll need to stay current on bankruptcy law; you'll need to read the recent cases and keep up with changes in the Bankruptcy Code; you'll need to keep your knowledge and skills sharp.

The same is true for legal writing.

Legal writing is like any skill or any substantive topic: there's always more to learn, and there's always room for improvement. Here's how.

Admit the truth.

When I was a full-time practicing lawyer, I thought I was a good writer. I believed I was above average within the profession. I was five years into my job as a legal writing teacher before I realized I hadn't been very good at all. I had been quite mediocre. I was poorly educated about the standards of high-level professional writing, and I was ignorant of my own limitations.

Was I unique?

Probably not. Many practicing lawyers believe themselves to be good writers, above average within the profession. I'll let you be the judge of whether most lawyers are above average. I'll simply say this:

The first step to becoming a good legal writer is to admit you have room to improve.

Get some references.

Once you've admitted you have room to improve your writing—that you still have things to learn—start learning. A great way to learn about writing is to consult the experts. When you have a question about writing, don't rely on half-remembered "rules" from high school English class. Look it up. But where?

The Internet works, and here are two websites I like:

- Purdue University's Online Writing Lab (OWL)
  http://owl.english.purdue.edu/
- Grammar Girl's Quick and Dirty Tips for Better Writing
  http://grammar.quickanddirtytips.com/

But if you're serious about legal writing, you should own some reference books, and here are three I recommend:

- *The Redbook: A Manual on Legal Style,* by Bryan A. Garner
- *Just Writing: Grammar, Punctuation, and Style for the Legal Writer,* by Anne Enquist & Laurel Currie Oates
- Texas Law Review *Manual on Usage and Style*

The idea is to have reliable references handy to answer questions: Do I need to capitalize appellant? How do I use the dash? Am I using shall (or which or ensure or infer or comprise) correctly? Plus, you inevitably increase your writing IQ whenever you serendipitously stumble upon an interesting entry.

Professional writers consult writing references, and you should, too.

Read the best books.

If you're really serious about improving, you'll have to do more than consult references. You'll have to study the principles of good writing and good legal writing. But how, when you're busy? Set a goal to read one book on writing every year. One per year. You can do that, right?

There are lots of good books on legal writing out there, and here are some I like:

- *Legal Writing Nerd: Be One* by Wayne Schiess
- *Point Made: How to Write Like the Nation's Top Advocates* by Ross Guberman
- *The Elements of Legal Style* by Bryan A Garner
- *Lifting the Fog of Legalese* by Joseph Kimble

These books are great sources of legal-writing knowledge.

Reading the best teaches you writing and exposes you to good writing.

Practice what you learn.

You're reading about writing and you're consulting writing references. You're becoming an informed legal writer. Now practice what you're learning.

Of course, for any working lawyer, writing practice is part of the job: you're writing all the time. Yet we all tend to rest on plateaus—we write in the same way we always have, with the same habits, the same mistakes. That's why studying writing is so important. Practice without study is just repetition. So experiment with things you're learning. Try new techniques and master new approaches to writing.

Through study and practice, you become a better editor of your work.

Drink deep of the substance.

One of the most common "writing" problems I see is the failure to understand what you're writing about. You won't write well if you haven't mastered the content. Yet many lawyers writing a legal analysis digest the authorities superficially; many doing drafting understand the transaction vaguely.

That's not good enough.

Why don't lawyers master their analytical and transactional content more thoroughly? Are they lazy? Probably not. Are they simply not up to the intellectual task? Not likely. Doubtless, it's that lawyers are always busy, under a deadline, and in a rush.

Don't let that be an excuse.

Gain a thorough understanding of your material. Read and re-read. Research and ask questions. Be sure you understand. Only when you understand the material can you write clearly and effectively, for example, by providing a strong summary. You will nearly always produce mediocre work when you are writing at the edge of your knowledge.

Gaining a thorough understanding does not mean delaying the first draft. Indeed, begin writing early, even before you have fully mastered the material. As you write, you'll gain understanding as well as begin realizing the gaps in your knowledge.

It naturally follows that starting the first draft shouldn't stop your study of the material. Let the writing and studying be recursive—return to each repeatedly. Continue to learn and continue to hone your text.

Content mastery is a condition to excellent writing.

Accept critique.

Now here's the hard part: seek and welcome critiques and candid suggestions for improving your writing. This one's tough because it's natural to be defensive about your writing—maybe even insecure. I know I am. But when I avoid critiques, I don't improve much. I rest on a plateau.

So open yourself up to honest critique. Find a trusted colleague, friend, or supervisor, someone whose judgment and writing you respect. Then ask for suggestions, and take them to heart.

The best writers are open to critique.

Summarize in everything.

Every legal document should begin with a summary of some kind. I mean everything: letters, memos, motions, briefs, reports, and even e-mail messages. This isn't my idea or a new idea, but it seems to be devilishly hard to implement. We all fall back on old habits and let writing inertia drag us along. A key to summarizing in every document is a good editing process—one in which you put yourselves in the place of a busy reader and ask, "What would I like to know, right up front?" Then write that. Besides, that kind of editing will help you, as a writer, focus on the key concepts.

Summaries aid readers—and writers.

Be clear and direct.

In all your legal writing, be as clear and direct as you can be while tailoring your writing to the audience. For example, when writing for nonlawyer clients, for typical consumers, or for the public, there is no call for jargon, obfuscation, or hyper-formalism. Likewise, when writing for a sophisticated audience, such as a supervising attorney, a judge, or opposing counsel, there is no need to simplify the text to a 7th-grade level. Instead, be as clear as your audience needs you to be, without over-simplifying.

Most lawyers have room for improvement in this area. For some reason, we legal writers tend to lapse into a formal, heavy writing style that has long sentences, big words, and excessive abstraction. Aim for a vigorous, direct style that relies on basic vocabulary when possible. For most legal writers, the work of making dense, complex writing clear will be done on the edit.

Strive to communicate, not to impress.

Now you're on your own. You're a professional legal writer, and I urge to take that job seriously.

Good luck.

Edit better.

We all understand that editing is a crucial part of the writing process. Most of us (and don't assume you're the exception) can't produce high-quality writing in one draft (or even two). We must edit, and here are some suggestions for doing it better.

First, leave plenty of time, even though it'll be hard to do. One expert on legal writing, Bryan Garner, has acknowledged that "the modern practice of law does not tolerate the type of revisory process necessary to produce a polished product."[2] That may be true, but you should still try to give yourself more time to edit. How much time? One pro recommends half the time on a writing project.[3] Can you afford that? Can your clients? It's up to you, but more editing means better writing.

Second, use more than one technique when editing:

- Do you edit on the computer screen?

That's fine, but it's not enough. Do some editing on a hard copy, too; we read and react differently to screen text and printed text.

- Do you read the text out loud?

That's great: you're using your ears, not just your eyes, to help you edit. Now go further and have a trusted colleague read it and suggest some edits.

- Do you read the document in reverse, from the last sentence to the first?

Good. This technique tricks your mind, so you're not familiar with the text; familiarity leads to poor editing. Now read only the topic sentences. Next read the opening and closing paragraphs.

Mediocre writing becomes good writing only through editing.

The Five-Pass Approach to Editing

With Elana Einhorn

You're past the hard part. You've created a logically structured analysis or argument supported by appropriate authority. You've revised it. You've incorporated any helpful suggestions from colleagues or clients. You now have a solid draft of your document, and you have some time for a careful edit. Before you embark on that edit, we have two suggestions.

---

[2] *Garner's Dictionary of Legal Usage* 533 (3d ed. 2011).
[3] Debra Hart May, *Proofreading Plain and Simple* 46 (1997).

First, edit in passes, focusing on one category of edits on each pass. Why? *Cognitive-load theory*, which is just a fancy way of saying your brain can do only so many things at once. The demands writing places on the brain have been studied and documented by Ronald Kellogg, a prolific researcher and the author of *The Psychology of Writing*.[4] Based on his research, we know that if you undertake an edit looking for everything—organization, sentences, word usage, punctuation, citation—you'll get a poorer result than if you focus on one category at a time. You might do a great job editing for punctuation and citation, but miss the organizational problems and weak sentences. Or you'll end up with a document in which the first half is well edited but the second half isn't. Your brain was just worn out.

Second, use an editing checklist. Again, relieve your brain of remembering everything you need to check. You should have a customized checklist suited to your own strengths and weaknesses and to the type of documents you write. But it's also a good idea to look for guidance.

Good checklists abound. Bryan A. Garner has a good one he calls the LawProse Editing Method, which appears in his book *Legal Writing in Plain English*.[5] Grammar Girl, Mignon Fogarty, has an excellent checklist online,[6] although it isn't geared toward legal writing and, as a result, focuses primarily on grammar and words. And one legal-writing professor, Megan McAlpin from Oregon, wrote an entire book, *Beyond the First Draft*, that is really a long, thorough editing checklist—with a chapter devoted to each "pass."[7]

---

[4] Ronald Kellogg, *The Psychology of Writing* 17, 201 (1994).

[5] Bryan A. Garner, *Legal Writing in Plain English: A Text with Exercises*, 163–64 (2d ed. 2013).

[6] 3 Mignon Fogarty, *Grammar Girl's Editing Checklist*, Grammar Girl's Quick and Dirty Tips, (Nov. 18, 2015, 10:00 a.m.), http://www.quickanddirtytips.com/education/grammar/grammar-girls-editing-checklist.

[7] Megan McAlpin, *Beyond the First Draft: Editing Strategies for Powerful Legal Writing* (2014).

Yet in reviewing the available checklists, we concluded that many are aimed at students. So we, a legal-writing teacher and an appellate lawyer, decided to produce our own checklist aimed at lawyers.

Here's a five-pass editing checklist that captures the essentials. It focuses on the things that matter most to the legal reader: accuracy and readability. These are potential issues that if left unaddressed might cause your reader—supervisor, client, judge or law clerk—to reread or stop reading altogether.

Overview
1. Edit for large-scale organization.
2. Edit for authority and citation.
3. Line edit for mechanics: grammar, punctuation, usage (words), and style
4. Edit for small-scale organization.
5. Print the document and edit the sentences.

Before You Start
Before you begin our five-step approach, you should have already taken advantage of any automated proofing features, including spell check. Did you know you can tell your software how to recognize party names and other unusual spellings that might appear in your document? You might also choose to run a grammar check, and if you do, check the box for "Show Readability Statistics" and, under "Settings" select your preferred grammar and style options.

1. Edit for large-scale organization.
If you use the Styles function in Microsoft Word, display the Navigation Pane or insert a Table of Contents to aid in this review. Then—

a. Identify the purpose of your document, and identify where in your document that purpose is made clear to the reader.

b. Be sure your document contains all the required parts.

   c. Review your main headings and subheadings, making sure that all headings at the same level are formatted and written consistently. Be sure they're enumerated correctly and consecutively.

   d. Be sure the sections of your document, as reflected in the main headings and subheadings, are in an appropriate order.

   e. Be sure the format and layout of your document conform to local rules, supervisor expectations, or client requirements.

2. Edit for authority and citation.
Make a decision about the importance of perfect citation form: abbreviations, spacing, typefaces, and so on.

   a. Be sure every factual or evidentiary assertion is supported by a citation to the record, docket, or evidence.

   b. Check every citation to the record, docket, or evidence and verify that it is accurate; check that all citations are consistently formatted and contain pinpoints.

   c. Be sure every legal assertion is supported by a citation to legal authority.

   d. Check every citation to legal authority and verify that it is bibliographically accurate; check that all legal citations are consistently formatted and contain pinpoints.

   e. Be sure every legal authority cited is current and binding or, if nonbinding, contains a concise statement of why it deserves weight.

   f. Assess the propriety of every string citation.

   g. Assess the citations and authorities as a hostile reader.

3. Edit for mechanics: grammar, punctuation, usage, and style.
Do this on a computer screen—a hard-copy pass is coming soon.

By "usage" we mean diction (word choice) and word usage (the difference between *effect* and *affect*). "Style" means the accepted conventions of professional writing: capitalization, typefaces, numbers, and symbols.

a. Read the document carefully, focusing on grammatical matters: verb agreement, verb tense, pronoun agreement, spelling, proper names (correctly and consistently spelled), capitalization, restrictives, modifiers, and any other mechanical matter you know is a problem for you.

b. Search for and verify the correctness of every apostrophe.

c. Search for and verify the correctness of every quotation mark.

d. Search for and verify the correctness of every colon and semicolon.

e. Search for and verify the correctness of every hyphen and dash.

You could also search for and verify the correctness of every comma, but we've tried it, and it's tedious.

4. Edit for small-scale organization.
That's the big picture; now be sure the ideas within that picture connect.

a. Be sure the document and each section in the document begin with the point (a summary, a conclusion, an overview, a roadmap).

b. Be sure that in every analysis or argument section, you introduce the controlling legal standards.

c. Be sure you accurately and succinctly describe any legal authority you plan to use. Edit for context, concision, and clarity. Assess whether you have over-used or under-used explanatory parentheticals.

d. Be sure every analysis or argument section applies the legal authorities—read as a hostile reader.

e. Read the opening sentence of every paragraph, verifying that each contains a clear connection to the previous paragraph and that each identifies the topic of the current paragraph. Check every numbered or bulleted list in the document for accuracy and consistency.

5. Print the document and edit the sentences.
Have a printed source to consult: a style reference for writing or legal writing. Use any trick necessary to objectively edit your own sentences: read it out loud, read it end to beginning, use a ruler, or put it aside for 24 hours or more.

a. Read the document and consider sentence length—any sentence taking up three or more lines of text or that makes you tired.

b. Read the document and look for excessive prepositions, unnecessary compound prepositions, redundancy, throat-clearers, misplaced modifiers, and unnecessary nominalizations.

c. Assess every passive-voice construction and if necessary, revise. (Microsoft Word's grammar-checker is good at spotting passive-voice constructions.)

d. Identify and justify every big word, formal word, and archaic word.

Finishing Up
Once you've completed these five steps, run one last spell check to look for any typos you might have created when editing. As you can see, this "five-step" approach has seven steps if you count running the spell check twice. But it's your work and represents your ability and credibility. So can you ever edit too much? The answer has to be no.

Advanced Topics
Mastering ...

Mastering the Colon

You could probably use more colons. They're handy: they can help you write concisely and briskly. The colon is a pointer, according to Bryan Garner in *The Redbook*, § 1.21. "Think of it as an arrow," he says. It introduces explanations, amplifications, and illustrations.

- The defendant has two choices: plead guilty or fight.
- Lasker got what the appellate team worked hard to obtain: remand for an evidentiary hearing.
- The merger agreement was like a puzzle: working it out was as rewarding as seeing it finished.

Of course, the colon introduces lists and quotations, according to June Casagrande in *The Best Punctuation Book, Period*. Those are some of the most common colon uses in legal writing.

A list

Summary judgment is inappropriate for three reasons:

(1) ...

(2) ...

(3) ...

A quotation

In *Carter v. Holland, Inc.*, the court refused to apply equitable tolling to state-agency filing deadlines, stating as follows:

[block quotation]

The text before a colon that introduces a quotation need not use "as follows," "the following," or similar phrase if the sense is clear. In fact, the colon itself often makes the sense clear. It says to the reader, "Hey, I'm about to quote something." Like this:

In *Carter v. Holland, Inc.*, the court refused to apply equitable tolling to state-agency filing deadlines:

[block quotation]

You need no colon after words like *including* and *such as*, and most consider it an error.

Not this

The defendant hired three lawyers, including: a transactional attorney and an appellate specialist.

But this

The defendant hired three lawyers, including a transactional attorney and an appellate specialist.

What can come before the colon in regular text? The traditional rule is that a colon should follow only an independent clause. Under that rule, these are wrong:

The testator stated:

The statute provides:

The attachments are:

The direct object or complement that would complete the thought is missing, so it's not an independent clause. That rule is why we often see these forms:

The testator made the following statement:

The statute provides as follows:

The attachments are the following:

This rule about independent clauses still applies in formal writing, especially if you know your reader is a punctuation traditionalist.

But the traditional rule is passing away in one context: you can ignore it in legal drafting when introducing numbered, lettered, or tabulated subparts.

The Lessee shall not: (1) paint, alter, or redecorate any portion of the Property; (2) change or install locks; or (3) place signs, displays, or other exhibits on the Property.

Or

The Lessee shall not:

(1) paint, alter, or redecorate any portion of the Property;

(2) change or install locks; or

(3) place signs, displays, or other exhibits on the Property.

What about capitalization? If what follows the colon *is not* an independent clause, do not capitalize the first word. If what follows the colon *is* an independent clause, capitalize the first word or don't, according to your preference, a house style guide, or office practice—but be consistent.

And finally, the colon is appropriate after the greeting or salutation in a formal letter:

Informal: Dear Sandra,

Formal: Dear Judge Haynes:

Mastering the Dash

The dash—it's good for breaks and pauses, emphasis and force.

The dash discussed here is the em dash. It's a long, horizontal punctuation mark—like these—and should be distinguished from the en dash – like these – a shorter mark used in number ranges and some types of compounds. On a typewriter, you create a dash by typing two hyphens with spaces on either side -- like that. Are you using a typewriter? Then don't use two hyphens. "Use real dashes," says Matthew Butterick in *Typography for Lawyers*.

To get the em dash in Word, type two hyphens, leaving no space on either side. Word should automatically convert that into an em dash. If you put a space before and after the hyphens, Word will convert that into an en dash, which is the wrong mark. You can also insert an em dash directly with the Insert Symbols function or with keystrokes: alt + 0151. On a Mac, hold down the Shift and Option keys and press the Minus key. Note that copying and pasting sometimes converts an em dash to a hyphen—a glitch you'll want to catch when you proofread.

Rules? The dash obeys few rules. It's flexible. You can use it in place of commas, colons, parentheses, periods, and semicolons.

In place of a comma:

> It was the seller who balked, not the buyer.

> It was the seller who balked—not the buyer.

In place of a colon:

> The courts assess three factors: purpose, type, and effect.

> The courts assess three factors—purpose, type, and effect.

A pair of dashes in place of a pair of commas or parentheses:

> Cally's statement, which was false, blamed the problem on Scoville.

> Cally's statement (which was false) blamed the problem on Scoville.

> Cally's statement—which was false—blamed the problem on Scoville.

The dash can even replace a period or semicolon, separating independent clauses:

Chen does not object to the fee. She asks that it not be disclosed.

Chen does not object to the fee; she asks that it not be disclosed.

Chen does not object to the fee—she asks that it not be disclosed.

With all these possibilities, how do you decide when to use a dash? Consider two key writing goals: breaks and emphasis.

According to June Casagrande in *The Best Punctuation Book, Period,* you can use the dash to indicate "breaks in a sentence" or "a change of sentence structure or thought." It signals a new direction, often abruptly, and might replace a heavier transition word:

Kaye will sell the yacht. However, the buyer must have financing within 30 days.

Kaye will sell the yacht—if the buyer has financing within 30 days.

Dashes also emphasize. In *The Redbook*, Bryan Garner calls the dash "a forceful and conspicuous punctuation mark." In the earlier example about Cally's statement, the paired parentheses downplay the inserted clause, the paired commas are neutral, but the paired dashes emphasize it.

Writers can use a single dash to point, and that pointing is emphatic. In the following examples, the second version highlights the lack of permission, and it's all in the dash:

Jeffrey deleted the paragraph without checking with his co-author.

Jeffrey deleted the paragraph—without checking with his co-author.

As for the myth: I've met lawyers and teachers who frown on the dash, saying it's too informal for legal writing. One legal-writing teacher told me he won't allow his students to use it. I disagree. The dash is entirely appropriate for legal writing, especially persuasive legal writing. Yes, overuse might be a problem, so exercise judgment, but you should add the dash to your writing tool kit.

Oh. And no more than two dashes per sentence, please.

Mastering Possessives

Here's an outline I'll use to discuss five possessive scenarios that can trip up legal writers:

1. possessives for words ending in *s*—singular (1a) and plural (1b)
2. joint possessives
3. possessives for possessive names
4. possessives for "plurals" that are singular
5. attributives

Here we go.

1a. To form the possessive of singular words ending in *s*, you have two choices—the journalism rule and the traditional rule. Under the journalism rule, if the word ends in *s*, even if it's a proper noun, just add an apostrophe outside the *s*:

- her boss' car
- a virus' impact
- Wayne Schiess' office
- Texas' policy

The journalism rule also applies to initials and to words ending in an *s* sound:

- the IRS' budget
- Xerox' revenue
- Gonzalez' salary

But under the traditional rule, add apostrophe + *s* even if the word already ends in *s* or an *s* sound:

- her boss's car
- a virus's impact
- Wayne Schiess's office

- Texas's policy
- the IRS's budget
- Xerox's revenue
- Gonzalez's salary

Which rule should you follow—the journalism rule or the traditional rule? I recommend the traditional rule, but ask your boss. Then be consistent. Consistency is more important than which rule you choose.

1b. Form the possessive for plurals ending in *s* or *es* by adding an apostrophe outside the *s*:

- her two bosses' cars
- all the viruses' impacts
- the Schiesses' house

2. When multiple nouns possess one thing, place an apostrophe + *s* after the last noun before the thing possessed. So *McCaffrey and Evans's lawyer* means the one lawyer who represents both. If they have their own lawyers—two lawyers, not one—then use apostrophe + *s* after both: *McCaffrey's and Evans's lawyers*.

3. To form possessives for entity names that are already possessive, like McDonald's and St. Anthony's, do we really write *McDonald's's shareholders* and *St. Anthony's's students*? No. The typical advice is to use *of* to write around the problem or to ignore the rules and leave the name unchanged. So—

- shareholders of McDonald's
- McDonald's shareholders
- students of St. Anthony's
- St. Anthony's students

4. Some nouns are singular but seem plural—the plural and singular forms are the same: American Airlines, United States, headquarters, and premises (meaning property). Form both the singular and plural possessive by adding an apostrophe after the *s*, like this:

- American Airlines' records
- the United States' tactics

- our headquarters' furniture
- the premises' fencing

If you're concerned about confusion, write around the problem: *the tactics of the United States, the fencing on the premises.*

5. It can be tricky to handle possessives for organization names and titles, like Farmers Market, Texas Mayors Association, and Veterans Day. Of course, they could be treated as plural possessives with apostrophes:

- Farmers' Market
- Texas Mayors' Association
- Veterans' Day

Follow the organization's lead, and if it uses an apostrophe, so should you. But if there's no clear answer, you can treat the name as attributive, not possessive. Attributives are nouns used as adjectives. So the market isn't possessed by the farmers; rather, the noun *Farmers* describes the market. And the Texas mayors don't own the association; *Texas Mayors* tells us what kind of association it is. Finally, Veterans Day doesn't belong to veterans in the sense of ownership; it's a day to honor them.

Ultimately, you can usually write around it, but it's also nice to know the rules.

Mastering Passive Voice

Do you know what the passive voice is? Some lawyers don't. Some think it is any verb that is not "strong," or any form of the verb *be*, or any past-tense verb. It is none of those, though all might be labeled "passive" in some sense.

Generally, it's a form of the verb *be* (*be, am, is, are, was, were, being, been*) and a past participle. (If the verb works with *have*, as in "have _____," then it's a past participle.) For example, in the sentence "I have baked," the word *baked* is a past participle. The word *written* is a past participle here: "I have written." When you combine a form of *be* with a past participle, you get the passive voice: *The pie was baked. The book was written.* A test. What's the passive voice here?

> The test might have been easier for students if it had been designed to measure their memories.

Remember, the passive voice requires a *be* verb and a past participle. *Been easier* is not passive voice; *easier* is not a past participle. The passive voice construction is *been designed*.

With the passive voice, the subject of the sentence isn't doing the action; the subject is being acted upon. And it's possible to leave the actor—the doer of the action—out of the sentence entirely. Thus, the passive voice has two natural consequences.

First, the normal reader expectation of *actor-action-thing acted upon*, which fits the typical English order of *subject-verb-object*, is altered. Instead, it becomes *thing acted upon-action-actor*. Or, because with passive voice you can leave out the actor, it can become *thing acted upon-action*. In other words, sentences can be in natural order, like *I sent the letter* or they can be in an atypical order, like *The letter was sent [by me]*.

Second, the passive voice tends to emphasize the thing acted upon. It removes the actor from the sentence or places the actor in a prepositional phrase at the end. So the passive voice affects emphasis in the sentence.

Both these consequences of the passive voice suggest legitimate uses. Lawyers may want to change the order of the actor and action in the sentence, emphasize the thing acted upon, obscure the actor, or eliminate the actor completely. For example, in the next sentence, the emphasis is on the letter, not on the sender:

> The letter was sent.

In the next sentence, the actor is intentionally hidden:

> The files were lost.

Using the passive voice in these ways is fine, as long as you do it intentionally and sparingly.

But the passive voice has drawbacks, too. When it includes the actor, it requires more words than the active voice, so it makes sentences longer. The passive voice is also dry and dull and can put readers to sleep. And when overused, the passive voice can seem evasive.

Better writers use the passive voice not mindlessly, as a default sentence construction, but deliberately and sparingly.

Mastering Nominalizations

Lots of legal writing contains nouns that could have been verbs. These nouns wanted to be verbs—they really did. But lawyerly habits and the default patterns of legal writing made these verbs into nouns

Only you can put them back.

Nouns that wanted to be verbs go by many names: *nominalizations*, *hidden verbs*, *buried verbs*. What you call them isn't important. What's important is that you learn to recognize when you've got nouns that could be verbs and train yourself to return them to their preferred state—unless you have a good reason to leave them as nouns.

This sentence contains two nouns that wanted to be verbs:

My expectation was that opposing counsel would make an objection.

If we return these nouns to their verb forms, the sentence improves:

I expected opposing counsel to object.

That example shows three benefits of using the verb forms in place of the noun forms.

By using verbs instead of nouns, you save words: the example went from 10 words to 6. You save words because using the noun requires you to add other words to help the noun. When you use the verb, you can cut the helpers, and that's fine because the helpers add little meaning,

By using verbs instead of nouns, you invigorate the text: the verbs in the revision are *expect* and *object*, which are forceful and strong; in the original, the verbs were *was* and *would make*, which are bland.

By using verbs instead of nouns, you focus on actions instead of on things or on status; this moves the writing along.

Your writing will be shorter, more vigorous, and more active if you let many of our nouns be verbs. But you don't have to take my word for it:

"Watch for and replace nouns created from stronger verbs." —Terri LeClercq in *Guide to Legal Writing Style*

"Use base verbs, not nominalizations." —Richard Wydick in *Plain English for Lawyers*

"Nominalizing is one of the most serious afflictions of legal prose, draining a sentence of vitality." —Tom Goldstein & Jethro K. Lieberman in *The Lawyer's Guide to Writing Well*

Now spot the two nominalizations in the next sentence:

The defendant made a referral to Emily Graves, a financial planner, so Graves could provide the plaintiff with advice.

The two nominalizations, along with their helpers, are *made a referral* and *provide … advice*. By using their verb forms instead, we lose the helpers, enliven the text, and focus on actions:

The defendant referred the plaintiff to Emily Graves, a financial planner, so Graves could advise the plaintiff.

When you write, spot the nouns that wanted to be verbs and, when you can, return them to their livelier verb form.

✦✦✦

Parallelism

Parallel Structure—Basic

Most legal writers know what parallelism is, but here's a review of the basics.

Parallel structure, or parallelism, means that when you write a series of items, phrases, or clauses, you follow two rules:

- Each item, phrase, or clause in the series flows naturally from the lead-in word.
- All items, phrases, and clauses in the series begin with the same part of speech.

For example:

> When editing a legal document, students should look for spelling errors, scan for punctuation mistakes, and proofread the citations.

Here, the lead-in is *should*, and these are the phrases in a series:

> look for spelling errors
>
> scan for punctuation mistakes
>
> proofread the citations

All three phrases in the series fit naturally with the lead-in word, and all three begin with the same part of speech—**verbs**:

> should ... **look** for spelling errors,
>
> ... **scan** for punctuation mistakes, and
>
> ... **proofread** the citations.

But this example has faulty parallel structure:

> When editing a legal document, students should look for spelling errors, punctuation mistakes, and proofread the citations.

The three phrases in the series do not all fit the lead-in word, and all three do not begin with the same part of speech:

should … **look** for spelling errors,

    … punctuation mistakes, and

    … **proofread** the citations.

Now, the second item in the series doesn't fit the lead-in and begins with a noun functioning as an adjective (*punctuation*). This is called *faulty parallelism*.

The longer the items in the series become, the more likely that you'll lose track of the lead-in word or of the part of speech used for the items. So managing the length of the items is good. No matter what, though, be sure your items in a series follow both rules.

Parallel Structure—Correlative

Another form of parallelism that advanced legal writers master is parallelism with correlative conjunctions. Here are the most-common correlative-conjunction pairs:

both … and

either … or

neither … nor

not only … but [also]

The basic rule is that the part of speech that follows the first conjunction should also follow the second; what follows *not only* should also follow *but also*. So A and B should be the same part of speech:

both A … and B

either A … or B

neither A … nor B

not only A … but also B

Thus, A and B must be syntactically identical: nouns, verbs, preposi-tions, adjectives, and so on.

Not this: Many lawyers are not only **smart** but also **work** hard.

Smart (adjective) and *work* (verb) are not the same part of speech.

But this: Many lawyers are not only **smart** but also **hard-working [diligent]**.

Another example:

The court was neither **willing** to look at the act of the owner in creat-ing a hazard, nor **at** the danger that customers created as they knocked items onto the floor.

The faulty correlative parallelism arises because *neither* precedes *willing* (participial adjective) and *nor* precedes *at* (preposition). Both these revisions are parallel:

The court was willing neither **to look** at the act of the owner in creat-ing a hazard, nor **to consider** the danger that customers created as they knocked items onto the floor.

The court was willing to look at neither **the act** of the owner in creat-ing a hazard, nor **the danger** that customers created as they knocked items onto the floor.

Parallel Structure—Fancy

Let's meet polysyndeton, asyndeton, and isocolon, three simple tech-niques of classical rhetoric—the effective and persuasive use of language. Don't let the fancy names put you off: you'll recognize these techniques, and you might be using them already. My own understanding of them comes from *Classical English Rhetoric*, by Ward Farnsworth (the Texas Law Dean) and from *The Elements of Legal Style*, by Bryan Garner.

Polysyndeton means using conjunctions between all the items in a se-ries. Although we normally write *The flag is red, white, and blue*, using polysyndeton we write *The flag is red and white and blue*. Thus, with polysyndeton we could write *The background check showed charges of vandalism and gambling and fraud and assault.* Or we could write *To improve your writing, you must study and practice and accept critique.*

In legal writing, polysyndeton can supply two types of emphasis. First, you emphasize each item singly. The extra conjunctions invite readers to think of the items separately rather than as a group. Second, polysyndeton tends to emphasize the sheer number of items in the list. Compare *The defendant's responses were hasty, terse, and superficial* with *The defendant's responses were hasty and terse and superficial.*

Asyndeton means omitting the conjunction, typically before the last item in a series. Although we normally write *The flag is red, white, and blue*, using asyndeton we write *The flag is red, white, blue.* Using asyndeton we could write *The background check showed charges of vandalism, gambling, fraud, assault.* Or we could write *To improve your writing, you must study, practice, accept critique.*

Asyndeton creates emphasis because omitting the conjunction isn't typical and is thus memorable. Although asyndeton can improve the rhythm of some sentences, it can also feel literary or even showy. Compare *The defendant's responses were hasty, terse, and superficial* with *The defendant's responses were hasty, terse, superficial.* In general, legal writers should use asyndeton cautiously.

Isocolon means a series of similarly structured phrases, clauses, or sentences of the same length. It's a form of parallelism. Although we might normally write *The flag is red and white, and it is also blue*, with isocolon we might write *The flag is red; it is white; it is blue* or *The flag is red. The flag is white. The flag is blue.* Using isocolon, we could write *The background check showed charges of vandalism, charges of gambling, charges of fraud, and charges of assault.* Or we could write *The background check showed charges of vandalism; it showed charges of gambling; it showed charges of fraud; it showed charges of assault.* Or this: *To improve your writing, you must confront your faults, practice your skills, and study others' writing.*

Using isocolon creates pleasant rhythms and allows writers to use a parallel structure to reinforce parallel substance. But consider this example: *The defendant's responses were inappropriate. They were hasty. They were terse. They were superficial.* The tone begins to sound oratorical. So although isocolon is appropriate for legal writing, it's more common in speech.

In fact, all three techniques appear more frequently in speeches and literature than in formal legal writing. Outside legal writing, all three can be used in more sophisticated ways than shown here. So as with any form of rhetoric and persuasion, be wise: before resorting to classical rhetoric, make sure your writing is clear and direct and correct.

Parallel Structure—Fancier

Here are anaphora, epistrophe, and chiasmus, three techniques of classical rhetoric presented in Farnsworth's *Classical English Rhetoric.*

Anaphora means repeating words at the beginnings of neighboring phrases or clauses. Although we might normally write—

> There is no doubt who committed the crimes: Mitchell hid under the stairs, assaulted Ms. Latham, and stole her purse.

Using anaphora we could write—

> There is no doubt who committed the crimes: Mitchell hid under the stairs, Mitchell assaulted Ms. Latham, and Mitchell stole her purse (repeats the subject).

> Although we might normally write—
> The Debtor repaid his wife, friends, and brother-in-law—but not the Bank.

using anaphora we could write—

> The Debtor repaid his wife, repaid his friends, and repaid his brother-in-law—but he did not repay the Bank (repeats the verb).

Anaphora creates emphasis through a sort of hammering. The repeated words are likely to be noticed and remembered. The repetition also creates expectations—the reader expects the pattern to be continued.

Because of that expectation, disrupting the pattern becomes an opportunity for emphasis, too. For example, in the sentence about the Debtor, repeating the verb *repaid* sets up the expectation that it will continue, but then the verb changes to *did not repay*, emphasizing the contrast.

Epistrophe means repeating words at the end of successive phrases or clauses. Although we might normally write—

The defendant followed, stalked, and harassed Mr. Taylor.

using epistrophe we could write—

The defendant followed Mr. Taylor, stalked Mr. Taylor, and harassed Mr. Taylor (repeats the object).

Although we might normally write—

Bennett illegally purchased, modified, and sold the rifle.

using epistrophe we could write—

Bennett's purchasing the rifle was illegal, his modifying the rifle was illegal, and his selling the rifle was illegal (repeats the predicate).

The hammering effect arises here as well, but it's more subtle because the repetition is evident only when the clause or item ends. Added to the hammering effect is the placement of the repeated words at the end—a natural place of emphasis. According to David Lambuth in *The Golden Book on Writing*, "The end is emphatic because it makes the last impression." Thus, epistrophe adds hammering repetition to the emphasis that naturally falls on a concluding word or phrase.

Chiasmus means repeating words or phrases in reverse order. It's inverted parallelism or an A-B-B-A pattern. A famous example: "Ask not what your country can do for you; ask what you can do for your country." The key words are *country* and *you*, repeated in this order: *country-you-you-country*.

Although we might normally write—

It was the defendant who stalked Taylor, not the other way around using chiasmus we could write—

> It was the defendant who stalked Taylor, not Taylor who stalked the defendant.

Instead of writing—

> Although the Bank has negotiated in good faith with the Borrower, the Borrower has not reciprocated.

using chiasmus we might write—

> Although the Bank has negotiated in good faith with the Borrower, the Borrower has not negotiated in good faith with the Bank.

Chiasmus may call attention to itself. It's a technique that might, in formal legal writing, come off as mildly pretentious. Thus, in *A Chiasmus and Contrast Can Help You Win*, lawyer Ethel Romm suggests that legal writers should use chiasmus with caution: "You should write at most one or two in a document." Yet a simple chiasmus can be quite memorable, as with this example from an appellate brief:

> State boundaries cannot extend beyond the national boundary. That would mean Texas was not annexed to the U.S., but that the U.S. was annexed to Texas.

Yes, caution is appropriate for all rhetorical techniques, but I recommend adding these three to your persuasive-writing toolkit.

✦✦✦

Sentences

Sentences: What's Average? What's Long?

What's a good average sentence length for legal writing? The experts say between 20 and 25 words:

- below 25—Wydick, *Plain English for Lawyers*
- about 22—Enquist & Oates, *Just Writing: Grammar, Punctuation, and Style for the Legal Writer*
- about 20—Garner, *Legal Writing in Plain English*

If you can push it into the teens, that's great. If you hit an average sentence length of 30 or more words per sentence, that's taxing for readers.

How do you know your average sentence length? Microsoft Word can tell you:

Click on File then Options then Proofing then When correcting spelling and grammar in Word. Now check the box for *show readability statistics*. You must also check the box for *Check grammar with spelling*.

Now each time you finish a spell check, you'll see a table displaying various data about your text. One thing you'll see is the average sentence length.

Note: The presence of headings and citations may drive the average sentence length down artificially. You can select a portion of text without headings or citations, or you can temporarily delete the headings and citations to get an accurate sense of your average sentence length.

You should try to vary your sentence length—some shorter, some longer—but how long is too long for any one sentence? My personal threshold is 45 words. When editing my own writing, if I read a sentence that seems long, I select it, note the word length and, if it's more than 45 words, I edit it.

Sentences: The Two Types of Run-ons

A run-on sentence isn't just a long sentence. A run-on sentence results from improperly joining independent clauses. Look at these two independent clauses:

> We understand there must be rules.

> Many forms of writing have rules.

They can't be joined like this:

> We understand there must be rules many forms of writing have rules.

That's a run-on sentence. But it's also incorrect to join two independent clauses with only a comma. When you do that, you create a type of run-on sentence called a *comma splice*:

> We understand there must be rules, many forms of writing have rules.

To properly join two independent clauses, you could use a semicolon, a comma with a conjunction (*and, or, for, nor, but, yet, so*), or a period (creating two sentences).

> We understand there must be rules; many forms of writing have rules.

> We understand there must be rules, and many forms of writing have rules.

> We understand there must be rules. Many forms of writing have rules.

There's another type of run-on sentence and it's trickier. It results from joining independent clauses with a conjunctive adverb and a comma. For example, this is a run-on sentence:

> Itemizing and attaching bills, therefore, constitutes prima facie evidence that medical charges were necessary and reasonable, however, there is still an issue of material fact to be considered.

The text contains two independent clauses:

> Itemizing and attaching bills, therefore, constitutes prima facie evidence that medical charges were necessary and reasonable.

There is still an issue of material fact to be considered.

But they've been improperly joined—or spliced—with a comma and a conjunctive adverb: *however*. Don't treat conjunctive adverbs as if they were conjunctions. If it helps, think of conjunctions as mere connectors and conjunctive adverbs as creators of transitions. In fact, they are often called "transition words." Here's a partial list of conjunctive adverbs:

accordingly	moreover
certainly	namely
consequently	nevertheless
finally	nonetheless
furthermore	similarly
hence	specifically
however	still
indeed	subsequently
likewise	therefore
meanwhile	thus

To fix the "conjunctive adverb" run-on sentence, you have at least three options:

Use a semicolon:

... charges were necessary and reasonable; however, there is still an issue

Use a conjunction instead:

... charges were necessary and reasonable, but there is still an issue

Make two sentences:

... charges were necessary and reasonable. However, there is still an issue

By the way, there's another conjunctive adverb in the original sentence (*therefore*), and it's set off with commas yet is correct:

Itemizing and attaching bills, therefore, constitutes prima facie …

Using the conjunctive adverb in this way is correct because it doesn't join two independent clauses. In short, "Itemizing and attaching bills" could not be a sentence by itself.

Learn to spot and fix run-on sentences, both the basic comma splice and the equally improper "conjunctive adverb" type.

Sentences: Danglers

In a sentence with a dependent, introductory modifying phrase, that phrase is deemed to modify the very next noun that follows it. When it doesn't, we imagine that the introductory phrase isn't connected to the rest of the sentence—it dangles.

Wrong: Speaking forcefully and passionately, the jury was swayed by defense attorney Juliet Anson as she made her closing argument.

- That example is a *dangling modifier* or *dangling element*. The introductory phrase (*speaking forcefully and passionately*) is meant to modify *defense attorney Juliet Anson*, but it actually modifies *the jury*.

Right: Speaking forcefully and passionately, defense attorney Juliet Anson swayed the jury as she made her closing argument.

Sometimes the introductory phrase is meant to modify a noun that is not just misplaced but is missing from the sentence:

Wrong: Having passed the bar exam, the swearing-in ceremony is next.

- Here, the introductory phrase begins with a present participle (*-ing* verb), so we have a *dangling participle*. The introductory phrase is meant to modify someone who has passed the bar exam, but that someone (a noun), is missing.

Right: Having passed the bar exam, you will attend the swearing-in ceremony next.

Sentences: Topic and Transition

Every piece of analytical legal writing (memo, report, advice letter, e-mail memo, motion, brief, CLE paper, whatever), needs a solid organizational plan. The order matters. But just as important as the order is the way you convey that order to the reader—the way you cue the order. Here are nine options for cuing order and creating transitions.

Before we get to the advice, a word about dates. Dates aren't topics. In reading memos, briefs, and other legal documents I notice that the facts often have three, four, or even five consecutive paragraphs beginning with a date:

On September 30, 2018, ...

On December 17, 2018 ....

On January 5, 2019 ....

And so on.

But it's good advice to omit a flurry of irrelevant dates: "Avoid over-chronicling—most dates are clutter." So says Judge Mark Painter in *The Legal Writer*: "We don't know what, if any, dates we should remember."

Even when dates are relevant, they're not the real topics. When you begin a paragraph with a date, you're saying the rest of the paragraph is about the date—or at least that the date is important. That's usually not true.

So if you need the date, see if you can avoid beginning with it. And if the specific date isn't important, you can use relative-time expressions:

Two weeks after the meeting ...

The next month ...

More than a year later ...

1. Use traditional transition words and phrases.

These are the classic transition words we all know. Grammatically, they're called *conjunctive adverbs*. A partial list:

- conversely, however, nevertheless, notwithstanding, on the contrary, on the other hand
- additionally, further, furthermore, moreover
- although, even though, though, whereas
- accordingly, in conclusion, finally, ultimately
- consequently, therefore, subsequently

2. Use short transition words.

Traditional transition words are great, but they can be a bit weighty; they're definitely formal. Sometimes you want a lighter touch, something crisp and vigorous. When you do, try these short transition words. The first list contains words that take a comma:

- also, besides, still, thus, what's more,

When used at the beginning of a sentence for transition, these words don't need a comma:

- but
- yet
- and
- nor
- or

3. Repeat content from the end of the previous paragraph.

Suppose your paragraph ends this way:

> The appellate court concluded that the disclaimer was conspicuous because it was in its own paragraph and in all-capitals text.

If you plan to add more information about all-capitals text, you could use *moreover* or *furthermore* or *additionally*. Or you could simply repeat the phrase *all-capitals text*, perhaps even making it the subject of the next paragraph's topic sentence, like this:

> All-capitals text alone might be insufficient if ....

Repeating the phrase cues the reader that you're on the same topic and have more to say about it.

4. Repeat the structure of the previous topic sentence.

If the topic sentences have similar structures, the paragraphs will feel connected. For example, imagine three consecutive paragraphs beginning with these three, similarly structured sentences:

> Using several strong formatting techniques will generally make a disclaimer conspicuous ...

> Using a single strong formatting technique can make a disclaimer conspicuous ...

> Using formatting techniques alone will not make a disclaimer conspicuous if ...

5. Adapt a key word from the end of the previous paragraph.

Instead of literally repeating a word from the end of the previous paragraph, you can adapt a word. One way is to take a verb from the end of the previous paragraph, nominalize it (make it a noun), and then make that noun the subject of the next paragraph's first sentence. Although over-using nominalizations can weaken legal writing, the technique has its appropriate uses, and this is one. For example, if a paragraph's last sentence says,

> Finally, the client **proposes** formatting the disclaimer in boldface type.

then the next paragraph might begin like this:

> The **proposal** would likely ...

6. Use subheadings.

Typical motions and briefs use subheadings, in the form of point head-ings, by convention or rule. But traditional memos can use subheadings, too—any document can. Subheadings ease skimming and provide cohe-sion. Most subheadings should be full-sentence explanatory or assertive headings rather than single-word or phrasal topic headings. For example, in a research memo, you might use a subheading like this:

a.   Senn can likely prove that Hamlin instructed her to commit the illegal act of Breach of Computer Security

And then, when the next topic arises, this:

b.   Senn was fired for the sole reason that she refused to perform the illegal act.

7. Use a demonstrative pronoun plus a noun.

Using a demonstrative pronoun (*this, that, these, those*) by itself can be vague: *This will not change the result* (what's *this*?). But if you follow the demonstrative pronoun with a specific noun, you can tie the current topic to a previous one. If the previous paragraph ended this way:

The appellate court concluded that the disclaimer was conspicuous because the text was formatted in all-capitals text.

the next paragraph might begin this way:

This single, strong format must still distinguish the disclaimer text from the surrounding text.

8. Use a single-sentence transition paragraph.

Yes, it's okay to write a single-sentence paragraph, if you do it deliber-ately and rarely. A single-sentence paragraph can be a great way to create an emphatic change of direction. Suppose you have two paragraphs with the following two opening sentences:

Using several strong formatting techniques will generally make a disclaimer conspicuous ...

Likewise, a single, strong format, such as all-capitals text, can be conspicuous.

You might then insert the following single-sentence transition paragraph:

Yet formatting techniques alone will not make a disclaimer conspicuous if there are other concerns.

The next paragraph would then discuss the other concerns.

9. Use ordinals.

Most of us met ordinals (first, second, third) in middle school as part of the five-paragraph essay. No, they're not too basic for legal writing if not overused. My suggestions:

- Use a set-up.
- Prefer bare ordinals (first, second) to adverbs (firstly, secondly).
- Prefer complete ordinal follow-through (first, second, third, fourth), avoiding *finally* (first, second, third, finally).

If possible, arrange a skim-able approach with the ordinals at the beginnings of paragraphs, like this:

[Set-up] In considering the format of disclaimer text that purports to be conspicuous, Texas courts have provided three clarifications.

First, using several strong formatting techniques will generally make a disclaimer conspicuous....

Second, a single, strong format, such as all-capitals text, can be conspicuous....

Third, the strong formatting must still distinguish the disclaimer text from the surrounding text....

✦ ✦ ✦

This Is Hard

This Is Hard: Don't Over-Delete *That*

Some writers recommend deleting *that* whenever possible, although it's hard to find the advice in a written source. Deleting *that* tightens the prose and speeds up reading, we're told. Sometimes. But deleting *that* can also slow down reading by causing momentary confusion. Here's an example:

Miscue:

> Mr. Li acknowledged being a minority made him more sensitive to discrimination.

> - Mr. Li acknowledged being a minority? We might think so for a moment. But then we read on and figure it out. Why confuse readers, even momentarily?

Better:

> Mr. Li acknowledged **that** being a minority made him more sensitive to discrimination.

> Try this example:

Miscue:

> The governor announced his new tax plan would be introduced soon.

> - For a moment, we think the governor announced his new tax plan. But no, not yet.

Better:

> The governor announced **that** his new tax plan would be introduced soon.

So scrutinize your *that*s. If deleting *that* will cause even a momentary miscue, leave it in.

This Is Hard: Restrictive Elements

Here we discuss three advanced grammar skills that require a knowledge of restrictive and nonrestrictive elements:

- restrictive and nonrestrictive appositives
- restrictive and nonrestrictive clauses
- restrictive and nonrestrictive participial phrases appositives

Restrictive and Nonrestrictive Appositives

An appositive is a noun or noun phrase that restates or renames another noun. Here, the noun Robin Lang restates or renames defendant:

The defendant, Robin Lang, did not hire a lawyer.

But properly punctuating appositives—using or omitting commas—depends on the type of appositive, and the type depends on whether the appositive provides information that is essential or additional.

The first type (essential) is called a *restrictive appositive* and doesn't need commas. This type of appositive renames or restates the noun in a way that is essential to a full understanding of the sentence. The appositive defines or restricts the original noun in a way that differentiates it from other nouns of that type. For example:

The politician Jordan Lopez gave the commencement address.

This sentence implies that there are multiple politicians and that the one who gave the commencement address was Jordan Lopez. That makes sense. If the appositive were set off with commas, it would create confusing implications:

The politician, Jordan Lopez, gave the commencement address.

This sentence implies that there is only one politician (in the world?) or that the politician is being differentiated from other nonpoliticians in some way. The commas are unnecessary.

Another example using my own name:

The dean asked Wayne Schiess the legal-writing teacher to edit the manuscript.

This sentence implies that there are multiple people named Wayne Schiess and that the dean asked one of those Wayne Schiesses—the one who is a legal-writing teacher—to edit the manuscript. So the sentence doesn't really make sense and should be punctuated like this:

The dean asked Wayne Schiess, the legal-writing teacher, to edit the manuscript.

That example is a *nonrestrictive appositive*. Nonrestrictive (also called "nonessential") appositives present what might be considered additional information, offered as extra or "by the way." You'd still have a sensible sentence without the appositive. Returning to our first example:

The defendant, Robin Lang, did not hire a lawyer.

The defendant [, whose name is Robin Lang, by the way,] did not hire a lawyer.

The defendant did not hire a lawyer.

Besides a pair of commas, you have other punctuation options for nonrestrictive appositives. If the restating phrase comes at the end of the sentence, use a comma and a period:

The party who did not hire a lawyer was the defendant, Robin Lang.

And you may set off appositives with a pair of parentheses, a pair of dashes, or a dash and a period:

The defendant (Robin Lang) did not hire a lawyer.

The defendant—Robin Lang—did not hire a lawyer.

The party who did not hire a lawyer was the defendant—Robin Lang.

A common mistake in using nonrestrictive appositives is failing to include the second comma:

Wrong: The defendant, Robin Lang did not hire a lawyer.

Wrong: Equitable adoption, a common-law doctrine may apply even in the absence of a court order.

The first example needs a comma after *Lang*; the second needs one after *doctrine*.

Properly punctuating appositives is a fundamental and basic skill in legal writing. It's something careful writers do well.

Restrictive and Nonrestrictive Participial Phrases

A present participle is an *-ing* verb, and it can introduce a nonrestrictive phrase. Legal writers should use a comma to set off a present participle that modifies an earlier noun and not the noun that immediately precedes it.

In other words, use a comma when the phrase applies to the earlier subject and not to the noun it follows.

Nonrestrictive phrase: Auden addressed the judge, asserting that the Equitable Tolling doctrine applied.

- The participle *asserting* modifies *Auden*, not *Judge*; Auden is doing the asserting, not the Judge, so the verb *asserting* needs a comma before it.

Restrictive phrase: Auden addressed the judge asserting that the Equitable Tolling doctrine applied.

- The participle *asserting* modifies *Judge*, not *Auden*; The Judge is doing the asserting, not Auden, so the verb *asserting* needs no comma before it.

In most sentences, the participle verb applies to the earlier noun, so the writer needs a comma.

Restrictive and Nonrestrictive Clauses with *Who*

Use a comma or commas to set off nonrestrictive relative clauses—groups of words that have a subject and a verb and that add parenthetical or additional information about a topic. Omit the commas if the clause is restrictive—it defines or limits the topic.

Here we discuss relative clauses using the pronoun *who*. The key to mastering these clauses is to develop a sense for when the clause is extra or "by the way" information (nonrestrictive, uses commas) and when the clause defines or limits something within a category (restrictive, no commas).

Nonrestrictive: The security guard, who was wearing sunglasses, pushed the plaintiff.

- This means there is one security guard and, by the way, that security guard was wearing sunglasses.

Restrictive: The security guard who was wearing sunglasses pushed the plaintiff.

- There is more than one security guard, and the one who pushed the plaintiff was wearing sunglasses.

Restrictive and Nonrestrictive Clauses: *That* and *Which*

Let's continue the discussion of restrictive elements with a thorough discussion of *that* versus comma + *which*.

It took me a year and a half, off and on, of reading about *that* and *which* to finally get it. The difference finally clicked when I realized this: comma + *which* adds extra information about an entire category, while *that* limits a modifier to part of a category.

The common mistake is to use *which* without a comma. And yes, it matters. Genuine ambiguity can result from failing to use *that* or comma + *which* correctly. Here's an example from Douglas Laycock's article *That and Which*:

The court always affirms damage judgments which turn on the facts.

Does this mean all damage judgments turn on the facts, and the court affirms them all (comma + *which*)? Or does it mean only some damage awards turn on the facts, and those are the ones the court always affirms (*that*)? We don't know.

The Board must approve all rental agreements which are subject to Section 4.

Does this mean all rental agreements are subject to Section 4, and the Board must approve them all (comma + *which*)? Or does it mean only some rental agreements are subject to Section 4, and those are the ones the Board must approve (*that*)? It's ambiguous.

That's why careful writers observe the difference between *that* and comma + *which*. The following examples helped me figure it out:

Nonrestrictive: The lawnmower, which is broken, is in the garage.

- There's only one lawnmower and, by the way, it's broken. This is extra information (broken) about the entire category (one lawnmower).

Restrictive: The lawnmower that is broken is in the garage.

- There are multiple lawnmowers, and the broken lawnmower is in the garage. This limits the meaning (broken) to part of a category (one of the lawnmowers).

If it's not clear yet, keep at it. Mastering the difference between *that* and *which* might take time and effort, but using them correctly will mark you as a careful writer.

This Is Hard: Compound-Modifier Hyphens

Take advantage of our new customer discount. This means a new discount for customers, but I bet the writer meant a discount for new customers. *We're selling a little used car.* This means the car is small, but I bet the writer meant the car had been used only a little. *He has a family law practice.* This means he practices with a relative, but I bet the writer meant he takes divorce cases.

What makes the meaning unclear in the examples is the absence of a hyphen. The rule—and yes, it's a rule of written English, although some of us never learned it—requires a hyphen between words that jointly modify a noun. Check out *The Chicago Manual of Style* § 7.85. These jointly modifying words are called *compound modifiers* or *phrasal adjectives.*

Careful writers hyphenate compound modifiers: *Take advantage of our new-customer discount. We're selling a little-used car. He has a family-law practice.* The hyphen clarifies meaning, letting the reader know, instantly, that the words modify the noun jointly, not independently. When the modifying phrase follows the noun, you need no hyphen: *We offer a discount to a new customer. The car we're selling is little used. His practice is in family law.* You also need no hyphen for proper nouns (*United States treaties*), foreign phrases (*prima facie case*), and adverbs ending in *-ly* (*highly skilled writer*). You do need a hyphen for *well* phrases, as in *well-pleaded complaint, well-known jurist,* and *well-rounded lawyer.*

Some legal writers doubt the rule and say they don't see compound-modifier hyphens in other writing. But the truth is they're everywhere. We don't notice them because they're doing their job—smoothing out our reading and eliminating miscues. For the skeptical, I offer a sampling of hyphenated modifiers from a single edition of the *Austin American-Statesman.* I recorded the first ten I saw:

single-family home

five-day period

technology-based processing system

city-owned street

since-discredited promise

60-vote majority

two-thirds requirement

far-reaching change

board-appointed reviewer

call-center jobs

If you look for them, you'll find compound-modifier hyphens in any well-edited publication.

But wait. There's more. You can use several hyphens if the modifying phrase has several words. So all the following are correct: *all-or-nothing trial strategy, on-the-spot investigation, two-year-old incentive deal.* But don't get carried away with long, hyphenated modifying phrases. This might be okay: *a sweep-it-under-the-rug approach,* but this is too much: *a let-the-jury-struggle-with-it-and-figure-it-out attitude.*

You can also use a "suspended hyphen" if you don't want to repeat the second part of paired compound modifiers. Instead of *right-brain and left-brain functions,* you can do this: *right- and left-brain functions. Or 15- and 30-year mortgages.*

In applying these hyphen rules, legal writers sometimes encounter a problem. In law, we have many familiar expressions and phrases that technically require hyphens but that will not confuse if left unhyphenated. For example, all these would take hyphens: *summary judgment motion, good faith requirement, reasonable person standard.* But hyphenating them can seem pointless and, given that some readers don't know the rule for compound-modifier hyphens, adding a hyphen might cause more confusion than it saves.

So you have a choice.

You can apply the hyphenate-your-compound-modifiers rule at all times, uniformly, even to familiar phrases. That way, you don't have to stop and think about whether you're causing confusion. You just follow your rule: I always hyphenate compound modifiers, and this is a compound modifier, so I'll hyphenate. Bryan Garner, in *Garner's Modern English Usage,* supports this "flat rule."

Or you can apply the hyphenation rule when confusion might result, but not to familiar legal phrases. So you'd hyphenate *high-performing employee* and *public-agency exception* but not *common law doctrine, third party beneficiary,* or *summary judgment motion.* Of course, with the case-by-case approach you have to gauge your audience's knowledge and differentiate general audiences from specialized ones. Thus, you'd probably need to hyphenate differently for a labor lawyer and for a generalist judge and maybe even for the judge's clerk. As you can see, you avoid wrestling with tough calls if you apply the flat rule.

Whether you apply the flat rule or a case-by-case standard, put "hyphenate compound modifiers" or "hyphenate phrasal adjectives" on your editing checklist.

✦ ✦ ✦

Typography

Typography: Basics

The way your documents look may not be the most important thing you worry about, and the way they look may be out of your control. But document-design principles for legal writing are changing—catching up to the rest of the writing world—and here are several key recommendations for lawyers.

Serifed font for body text. Serifed fonts, so called because of the small extensions or "serifs" on the strokes, look professional and are easy to read when printed: Cambria, Georgia, and Century Schoolbook (used in this book). Times New Roman is the most common serifed font in legal writing, but typography expert Matthew Butterick says, in *Typography for Lawyers*, that because it was designed for narrow newspaper columns in small font sizes, it isn't good for legal documents at larger font sizes. And all the experts say to avoid Courier.

Same serifed font for point headings. Explanatory headings, also called point headings and subheadings, are complete sentences that state or assert a point. (A point heading in a motion or brief is a type of explanatory heading.) They should be in the same font as the body text (serifed) but should use bold, bold italics, or italics to make them stand out.

Sans serif font for short, topic headings. Sans serif fonts lack serifs and look slightly less formal than serifed fonts. I like the boldface versions of Calibri, Corbel, and Verdana. Arial is a common sans serif font that many experts dislike. When you use a boldface sans serif font for short, topic headings, the contrast with the serifed body text will make the headings stand out and make the document easier to skim. This approach is entirely appropriate for court documents, memos, and transactional documents. I follow this approach in this book.

Spacing. Double line-spacing, an unfortunate tradition in legal writing, makes documents hard to skim, uses up twice as much paper, and actually slows down reading. Think of the reading you do outside the law: newspapers, magazines, and books. None is double-spaced. So unless required by rule or by your boss, avoid double-spaced text.

But use single-spacing wisely. A single-spaced document in an 11- or 12-point font with 1-inch margins is crowded. Adjust your settings: increase the spacing to 1.1 or 1.2, increase the font size, or push the margins in to 1.3 inches.

Centering. Never center the body text and, despite common conventions, you would do well to avoid centering headings and subheadings. Left-aligned headings look neater and are easier to skim.

For more tips on document design, check out *Typography for Lawyers* by Matthew Butterick and *The PC is Not a Typewriter* by Robin Williams.

Typography: Justification

For legal documents, some lawyers prefer justified text (also called "fully justified" text) and others prefer left-aligned text (also called "left-justified" text). Fully justified text creates clean, vertical margins on the left and right, while left-aligned text creates a clean left margin and a ragged right margin.

Which is better? The question sparks passionate debates. I think either is fine for legal documents, and here I describe the pros and cons of each and then offer some recommendations.

Fully justified text produces neat, vertical margins that create the sense of a line on each side of the document. Justified text thus tends to look formal and serious, and that's why professionally printed documents are often fully justified. For example, nearly all books use justified text (this one does, too). I just looked through ten random books in my office: the text is fully justified in every one. I looked through five magazines I have on hand: four use full justification throughout.

But the full justification that looks neat and professional to some looks dry and uninviting to Matthew Butterick, author of *Typography for*

Lawyers. He doesn't fully justify the text in his legal documents (he's primarily a trial lawyer). He says full justification "is not a signifier of professional typography."[1] And Bryan Garner, in *Garner's Dictionary of Legal Usage*, reports on readability research showing that fully justified text is harder to read than left-aligned text.

Left-aligned text produces a ragged right margin that looks less formal. Butterick says left-aligned text relaxes the look. Most websites (all ten I checked) and informal correspondence (think email) are left aligned, and even some professional documents are left aligned. One of the magazines in my office uses left-aligned text, and the *Austin-American Statesman* left aligns its text—ragged right margins throughout.

But the left-aligned text that looks relaxed to some looks messy and unprofessional to others. After all, a ragged right margin is a vestige of the typewriter, which couldn't produce fully justified text. Once upon a time, only professional printers could fully justify text. Now, with word processors, we can all easily justify our text and give it the look of a professionally printed document. After all, why would you want your text to look like typewriter text?

Yet it's the word processors (like Microsoft Word) that are the problem, says Butterick. "The justification engine in a word processor is rudimentary compared to a professional page-layout program."[2] So the fully justified text in the books we read looks great, but we all know justified text in a Word document often has unsightly gaps and spaces. The "rudimentary" justification engine is struggling to stretch and condense your text to fit the line length. It's those gaps and spaces, by the way, that make fully justified text less readable.

So if you like justified text—the neat vertical margins—go ahead and justify. But if you're not using a sophisticated publishing program, you should turn on hyphenation. In Word 2010, go to Page Layout > Hyphenation. This function breaks words at the right margin (as some of us used

---

[1] Matthew Butterick, *Typography for Lawyers* 136 (2010).
[2] *Id*.

to do on a typewriter—remember?). Turning on hyphenation gives Word another tool to help the text fit the line length, and it reduces gaps and spaces. You should probably choose automatic hyphenation, not manual, and look through the other hyphenation options. And note that the function isn't perfect: in a document I was preparing, Word once hyphenated newsletter as new-sletter. You have to proofread.

The text in this book in fully justified with hyphenation.

If you dislike justified text—the gaps and spaces—or if you don't care, go ahead and use left-aligned text with a ragged right margin. According to Butterick and Garner, left-aligned text is appropriate for legal documents.

Typography: Effective Headings and Subheadings

Nearly every legal document can benefit from clear, consistent headings. The guidelines here are particularly useful for memos, motions, and briefs. In this section I describe two kinds of headings, give typeface advice, and offer suggestions for placement and alignment. Next, I offer recommendations for making headings consistent, commend some traditional outlining rules, and suggest a simple numbering system. These guidelines should help you create readable, skim-able documents.

Topic Headings

I use "topic heading" for single-word or short-phrase headings that identify topics, like Argument, Discussion, and Statement of Facts. Because a topic heading isn't a complete sentence, it doesn't take a period, and you typically capitalize each main word (Initial Caps). I use the mnemonic C-A-P to remember to capitalize everything but conjunctions, articles, and prepositions. The heading above the previous paragraph is a topic heading.

Topic headings should stand out from the body text, and here are three options. (1) Use boldface. Yes, ALL-CAPITALS and underlining are common for topic headings, but if you follow modern typographic principles, you'll avoid them: they impede reading and are vestiges of the typewriter. (2) Make topic headings slightly larger than the body text by 1 or

2 points, then add boldface. (3) My preference: Use a contrasting font. If the body text is in a serifed font like Cambria, Garamond, or Century Schoolbook—and it probably should be—then topic headings in a sans-serif font like Calibri, Tahoma, or Verdana will really stand out.

Topic headings designate the major sections of a legal document. For example, in a motion for summary judgment, the topic headings might be Introduction, Statement of Facts, Motion Standard, Argument, and Relief Sought. Because of their nature and the way they're displayed, they don't require numbering.

Topic headings are often centered, but it's not a rule, just a common convention. Knowing, as we do, that many readers will read our documents on a screen, and knowing that screen readers have a top-left viewing preference and skim a lot, it makes sense to put topic headings on the left margin. That's what I do.

Legal documents often use point headings.
I use "point heading" or "explanatory heading" for the full-sentence headings and subheadings that break up a discussion or argument. The persuasive point headings in motions and briefs are the most common type, but lawyers use non-persuasive point headings, too. I used one for this paragraph.

If a heading is a complete sentence, and point headings generally should be, then it takes a period. If it's a sentence, use sentence case, capitalizing only the first word. DON'T SHOUT AT THE READER WITH ALL-CAPITALS, and Avoid Using Initial Caps For Explanatory Headings Because It Looks Odd.

A good way to make point headings stand out is to use the same font as the body text and add emphasis with boldface, bold italics, or italics. With those three typefaces, you could have three outline levels beneath your topic headings. Generally, place the first-level explanatory heading on the left margin and indent each lower level one more tab length.

As you format explanatory headings, keep these tips in mind. (1) Avoid over-indenting. If you indent more than three tab lengths, you spoil the left-alignment screen readers and skimmers prefer. (2) Keep explanatory headings to three outline levels if possible. It simplifies things for the reader and helps prevent over-indenting. (3) Use indentation, not mere tabbing, so subsequent lines of text align with the first.

Another type of heading. A third type of heading is the inline or "run-in" heading, like the one I used in this paragraph. It's not a sentence but still takes a period, and it is emphasized with boldface.

Generally, your headings should form an outline, and in outlines, entries at the same level should be structured and formatted the same way. That may seem obvious, but not all legal writers do it, as I recently realized when reading motions and briefs in preparation for a CLE seminar.

For example, suppose the Argument portion of a motion or brief has the following heading outline: 1. a. b., 2. a. b. In that outline, headings 1 and 2 are at the same level, so they should be structured and formatted the same way. Likewise, both a-b pairs are at the same level, so all four should be structured and formatted the same way.

Specifically, if heading 1 is a topic heading in boldface initial caps, then 2 should be a topic heading in boldface initial caps. If 1a and 1b are full-sentence, explanatory headings in bold italics, then 2a and 2b should also be full-sentence explanatory headings in bold italics.

Poor formatting:

1.   Trial Court Errors

    a.   The trial court erroneously instructed that police officers may pretend to be electors.

    b.   The trial court failed to have the court reporter record statements made on audio recordings.

2.   Sufficiency of the Evidence

    a.   Sufficiency of the evidence on attempted election bribery.

    b.   Sufficiency of the evidence on conspiracy to commit election fraud.

Better formatting:

1.   Trial Court Errors

    a. The trial court erroneously instructed that police officers may pretend to be electors.

    b. The trial court failed to have the court reporter record statements made on audio recordings.

2. Sufficiency of the Evidence

    a. The evidence on attempted election bribery was insufficient.

    b. The evidence on conspiracy to commit election fraud was insufficient.

The structure of 1a and 1b (full sentences) doesn't match the structure of 2a and 2b (phrases). So revise 2a and 2b into full-sentence, explanatory headings. The format, bold, should match, too. Finally, use hanging indentations.

Outline consistently. In creating headings and subheadings, follow two key outlining rules.

Rule 1: Keep main topics at the same level and keep subtopics at the same, lower level. Thus, at a single outline level, don't place main headings and subheadings. Consider the next example.

Poor outlining:

1. **Preliminary Statement**
2. **Argument**
3. **The Plaintiff Cannot Prove Consequential Damages.**
4. **The Plaintiff Cannot Prove Expectation Damages.**
5. **Conclusion**

Better:

1. **Preliminary Statement**
2. **Argument**
       a. *The plaintiff cannot prove consequential damages.*
       b. *The plaintiff cannot prove expectation damages.*
3. **Conclusion**

Rule 2: Don't create a subheading unless you have two. If you have only one subheading, incorporate it into the main heading. (If your argument or discussion contains only one major issue, it's okay to have a single major heading for that issue.) For example—

Poor outlining:

    a.   The suit is barred by laches.

        (1) The suit was brought twenty-five years after the original certificate was issued.

Better:

    a.   The suit is barred by laches because it was brought twenty-five years after the original certificate was issued.

Number consistently. Traditional outlines begin with Roman numerals (I, II, III) and proceed through letters (A, B, C, and a, b, c) and Arabic numerals (1, 2, 3). If you supplement those levels with romanettes (i, ii, iii), and parentheses ((a), (b), (c) and (1), (2), (3)), you can create an outline with seven levels: I. A. 1. a. (1) (a) (i)

But first, don't write a document (motion, brief, or even a contract) that needs seven outline levels. Find a way to condense and consolidate; strive to limit yourself to four or even three levels.

Second, if any level of your outline will go beyond nine or ten entries, consider using Arabic instead of Roman numerals. Roman numerals get harder to decipher the higher they go. I once read a lengthy contract divided into 60 sections, each designated with a Roman numeral. It was hard to refer to any particular article because it took too long (or became impossible) to figure out. What's XLIV? In my own outlines, I use Arabic numerals and the alphabet, and I still have four levels available: 1. A. (1) (a).

It's 44 by the way.

✦ ✦ ✦

Plainness

Plainness: What is Plain English?

How should we define plain English for legal writing—or what are its traits? What kinds of legal text should be in plain English? And how do we do it? I try to answer these questions here.

In defining plain-English legal writing, let's start with a first principle: legal writing is audience-focused. All legal writing should be appropriate for its audience—it should communicate with the intended reader in words, sentences, and forms the reader can understand.

Yet we have to acknowledge that most legal writing has multiple audiences. For example, a brief might be read by a judge, the judge's clerks, opposing counsel, and others. A contract might be read by counsel on the other side of a transaction, the client, and others. Writing effectively for multiple audiences is difficult, so my assertion that legal writing should be audience-focused was an oversimplification. I'll modify the advice: legal writers should write for their "primary audience."

If the primary audience for a particular legal document is non-lawyers, we arrive naturally at a good definition of plain-English legal writing: it's legal writing that can be read and understood by non-lawyers.

With that definition in mind, can we identify the specific traits of plain-English legal writing? You can find many definitions; they're all over the Web, and writers have produced many books on the subject. Those who have tried to legislate plain English have created definitions, too. A New York statute contains this simple definition. Certain consumer legal documents must be, "Written in a clear and coherent manner using words with common and everyday meanings."

Other plain-English legislation, in Pennsylvania and Connecticut, for example, contains lists of 10 to 15 specific attributes, like "uses short sentences and paragraphs," "uses personal pronouns," and "uses simple and active verb forms." Some states require a certain numerical score on the Flesch Reading Ease scale—a scale of 0 to 100 that relies on word length and sentence length and that's available on Microsoft Word. The higher the score, the plainer the text. Florida's numerical requirement is 45 out of 100, and Texas's is 40, although Rudolf Flesch said, *In How to Write Plain English*, that plain English requires a score of at least 60.

Beyond legislation, writing experts have produced plain-English guidelines. Joseph Kimble has an excellent, exhaustive list in his book *Lifting the Fog of Legalese*, for example. I have my own guidelines, adapted from my own book on the subject, *Plain Legal Writing: Do It*:

1. Assume an audience untrained in the law and that prefers easy reading.
2. Design readable text: manage type, lines, and layout.
3. Design accessible documents: use summaries, headings, and numbering.
4. Prefer everyday language.
5. Prefer active and direct words, sentences, and constructions.
6. Abandon legalisms, archaisms, and Latinisms.
7. Consider using "we" and "you"; consider using contractions.
8. Manage sentence length to come under a 20-word average.
9. Manage paragraph length for digestible chunks.
10. Test documents on readers.

I hope you'll agree that the principles of plain English are sensible and not complex.

But revising legal text into plain English is taxing, tedious, and slow. The resulting plain-English only looks like it was easy to write. In reality, the process has several steps and usually requires collaboration. For example, here's a process I recommend, also taken from my book, *Plain Legal Writing: Do It*:

a. read the entire document from beginning to end—taking notes—to get a sense of the content and complexity;
b. create a list of the document's content to use as a checklist when you revise;

   c. sort and order the content list, considering reader needs, importance of topics, and the order of events in the transaction—and begin thinking about headings, subheadings, and numbering;

   d. rewrite the text in plain English;

   e. revise and edit the text;

   f. test the text on intended users and ask others to read and comment on the text—your other readers should include at least one lawyer who is an expert on the subject matter and at least one nonlawyer unfamiliar with the subject matter.

As you can see, revising legal text into plain English could be time-consuming and difficult. But for certain documents, it's worth it to have the audience understand.

So where does Plain English belong? What documents should be written in plain English? It's a broad category I call consumer legal documents. Unlike most briefs and business contracts, which are intended for lawyers, consumer legal documents are intended for nonlawyers:

Credit-card agreements

Product disclaimers

Car loans

Bank-deposit agreements

User agreements

Insurance policies

Apartment leases

Mortgage applications

Website-user agreements

And more. They should be written in plain English. Yet many are not.

Too many consumer legal documents with legal content that creates rights and duties are still written in dense, complex prose. The layout is crowded, the sentences are long, and the vocabulary is complex. We can do better. Here are some examples of true plain English some legal writers are creating and using today.

From the Texas Office of the Consumer Credit Commissioner:

Before

For value received, the undersigned borrower(s) promise(s) to pay to the order of XYZ Loan Company, 123 Main Street, Anytown, Texas, 77777, at the above address the amount shown above as the Total of Payments.

After

I promise to pay the Total of Payments to the order of you, the Lender. I will make the payments at your address above.

From the Texas jury instructions in Texas Rule 226a:

Before

It may become necessary for another jury to re-try this case with all of the attendant waste of your time here and the expense of the litigants and the taxpayers of this county for another trial.

After

I might have to order a new trial and start this case over again. This would waste your time and the parties' money, and would require the taxpayers of this county to pay for another trial.

From the Veteran's Administration:

Before

Persons eligible for death benefits include any citizen of the United States who, during any war in which the United States has or may be engaged, served in the Armed Forces of any Government allied with the United States during that war, whose last active service was terminated honorably by death or otherwise, and who was a citizen of the United States at the time of entry into such service and at the time of death.

After

You may be eligible for death benefits if:

- you served in the U.S. Armed Forces or of one of our allies in any war we fought;

- your last active service ended honorably, and

- you were a citizen of the U.S. when you entered the service and will be at your death.

These texts are true plain English—legal content nonlawyers can understand.

Plainness: The Formality Continuum

Sources on legal-writing style often advise writing plainly, being direct, and using shorter, common words in place of longer, obscure ones. In *Legal Writing in a Nutshell*, the authors (Bahrych, Merino, & McLellan) say "a plain style is usually the best style." Plain English, according to Mark Cooney in *Sketches on Legal Style*, "isn't plain at all, if by that you mean dull and drab. It's refreshing, persuasive, interesting." And in *The Art of Advocacy*, Noah Messing urges us to "use the simplest term that meets your needs."

I often approach this advice not from the perspective of simplicity and plainness, but of formality and informality. It may be just another way of describing the same thing, but I've found that it helps some legal writers, including me, to think about word choice as falling along a continuum:

Informal   *Formal*

<————————————>

So instead of saying that *help* is a small word and *assist* is a big one, I say that *help* is an informal word and *assist* is a formal one—it's closer to the formal end of the continuum.

The formality continuum I'm discussing is for professional legal writing: work-related email, professional correspondence, legal filings, court pleadings, and other legal documents. Your personal text messages, social-media posts, and other similar writings are on a separate continuum. Speech is on another. What I'm talking about here is the continuum for legal writing.

For almost any idea or concept, legal writers can choose words that fall near the informal or formal end of the continuum. For example—

Informal	Formal
ask	request
build	construct
start	commence
teach	educate

And so on.

Similarly, using *and* or *so* to begin a sentence falls near the informal end of the continuum, whereas using *additionally* and *therefore* is more formal. And using contractions in a legal document would be informal, while avoiding them would be more formal.

Informal	Formal
And	In addition, Additionally
So	Therefore, Thus
can't	cannot

Here are two examples, formal and informal:

Formal

Additionally, the judgment against Hunter cannot stand because the economic-loss rule bars the negligence claim. Therefore, the judgment should be reversed.

Informal

And the judgment against Hunter can't stand because the economic-loss rule bars the negligence claim. So the judgment should be reversed.

You can also move along the formality continuum with phrases, particularly a structure called a *nominalization*—a noun that could have been a verb.

Informal	*Formal*
help	provide assistance to
settle	enter a settlement

A benefit of thinking about word choice this way is that we get away from wrong or right. Using contractions and beginning with *and* aren't wrong; they're informal. For many legal writers, those choices would be too informal for an appellate brief, but would be fine for email.

Now the advice.

First, be aware of the formality continuum in your professional writing, and use the appropriate level of formality for the context—the type of document and the audience. Certainly most legal writers are doing this already.

Second, when you can, move your writing toward the informal end. Utilize the base verb in lieu of the nominalization. *Use the base verb instead of the noun.* Make a selection in favor of the Anglo-Saxon term rather than the Romance term. *Choose the Anglo-Saxon word in place of the Romance word.* Your readers will appreciate it.

Plainness: Saxon Words and Romance Words

In reading about writing, I've run across the following advice, here from H.W. Fowler:

> "Prefer the Saxon word to the Romance."[3]

And here from Strunk & White:

> "Anglo-Saxon is a livelier tongue than Latin, so use Anglo-Saxon words."[4]

But I never paid much attention because I didn't know what it meant. When I finally learned, I saw that the advice could apply to legal writing, too. Here I give some background, offer some recommendations, and suggest some new techniques.

Two key sources of English words are Anglo-Saxon and Latin; many words of Latin origin are also French and are sometimes referred to as being of "Romance" origin.[5] Yes, I'm skipping the history lesson, but some common examples can help make the point. Here are four paired synonyms or near-synonyms; the first is of Anglo-Saxon origin and the second is of Latin/French/Romance origin:

- break/damage
- come/arrive
- make/create
- need/require

We can now make some generalizations. Saxon words tend to be shorter—often single-syllable—and harder in sound. They also tend to be concrete rather than abstract and less formal, too. We might say that Saxon words are plain and that Romance words are fancy:

- boss/superior

---

[3] H.W. Fowler, *The King's English* 1 (1906).
[4] William Strunk, Jr. & E.B. White, *The Elements of Style* 77 (4th ed. 2000).
[5] Ward Farnsworth, *Classical English Style* (forthcoming).

- job/position
- wish/desire
- lawyer/attorney

Test yourself: Name the Romance near-synonym for these Saxon verbs: *ask, buy, eat, see, talk.*

What can we do with this knowledge? Replace Romance words with Saxon words—although not always. The best writing advice is rarely "always" or "never." Instead, generally choose Saxon words but use your editorial judgment, considering audience, tone, persuasion, and legal terms.

Consider these before-and-after examples taken from appellate briefs.

Before: The City Planner agreed that Hemet's lot was *adjacent to* the single-family homes.

After: The City Planner agreed that Hemet's lot was *next to* the single-family homes.

This is a sensible edit that substitutes a shorter Saxon word for a longer Romance word, making the text a bit more readable.

Before: Mr. Castillo asserts that Ms. Castillo has no constitutional right to the effective *assistance* of counsel in a divorce suit.

After: Mr. Castillo asserts that Ms. Castillo has no constitutional right to the effective *help* of counsel in a divorce suit.

Probably not a good edit. "Effective assistance of counsel" is a standard legal phrase. Don't replace Romance with Saxon when the Romance term is, or is part of, standard legal language.

Before: The judge erroneously allowed the testimony and then permitted the jury to *cogitate* on it overnight.

After: The judge erroneously allowed the testimony and then permitted the jury to *think* about it overnight.

This is a solid edit. The original, with *cogitate*, gives an archaic or crusty sense to the text. *Think* is better.

"But wait," you might be saying. "I can achieve the same clarity and force in my writing just by using a short word in place of a long one. How does it help me to know that the short words are Saxon and the long ones are Romance?"

I hope it helps in two ways. It raises your writing IQ, something that I believe lawyers, as professional writers, should seek. And that knowledge can lead to other insights based on the Saxon/Romance distinction, which we'll discuss next.

Saxon Words and Romance Words in Contracts

We've now learned a new way to think about plain words versus fancy ones: sometimes it's the difference between words of Saxon versus Romance origin. To set the stage for this section, try this: For each Saxon-named animal, give the French (Romance) name for the type of meat: *chicken, cow, deer, sheep, pig.*

Now think about contracts and other binding legal documents. You may have noticed that they often contain what we now know are Saxon-Romance pairs:

agree and covenant

cease and desist

due and payable

hold harmless and indemnify

sell and convey

true and correct

will and testament

Why?

During the 1200s, French became the primary language of the law in England. In the 1400s and after, English began to replace French as the language of the upper classes. (History lesson omitted.) Hence the Saxon names for animals and the Romance names for their meat when served— as seen in our quiz.

But English also began to replace French as the language of the law. Thus, as explained by David Crystal in *The Stories of English*, legal scribes often had to decide what words to use when "French and English each provide a copious supply of relevant items."[6] Often they didn't choose—they used both.

As Crystal puts it, "Old English *goods* and Old French *chattels* resulted in Middle English legalese, *goods and chattels*."[7] Sometimes the pairs were synonyms, sometimes they were subtly different, and sometimes they were paired out of habit or for other reasons.

Many of these doublets persist today, as we see in the pairs listed above. We also see triplets:

- give, devise, and bequeath
- ordered, adjudged, and decreed
- right, title, and interest

Old legal language isn't necessarily bad legal language, so how should legal drafters address these doublets, triplets, and longer strings? My advice here relies on my preference for plain, direct words and on the expertise of Kenneth Adams in his *Manual of Style for Contract Drafting*.[8]

First, do enough research to decide whether the doublet, triplet, or string contains words that differ in meaning or whether they're true synonyms. (Sources to consult: Adams's *Manual of Style*, Garner's *Dictionary of Legal Usage*, and *Black's Law Dictionary*.) If they're not true synonyms, decide which meanings you intend and keep only the words you need.

Second, if you have true synonyms, do your best to pick one word that conveys your intended meaning and delete the others. For example, in

---

[6] David Crystal, *The Stories of English* 152 (2004).
[7] *Id.*
[8] Kenneth A. Adams, *A Manual of Style for Contract Drafting* 6-7 (3d ed. 2013).

most contracts, *sell and convey* can be shortened to *sell*. If you intend separate actions—selling the item and then conveying it to the buyer—then separate provisions requiring the seller to both sell the item and deliver it would be better.

What about the stock judicial phrase *ordered, adjudged, and decreed*? Yes, it's harmless as is, but shortening to *ordered* would also be harmless.

And this monster is still sometimes used with security interests: *grant, assign, convey, mortgage, pledge, hypothecate* [what?], *and transfer*. Adams says that it can be shortened to *grant*.[9]

To those who say that the extra words are harmless, so there's no reason to remove redundancies, I can say only this: you're mostly right. But the best writers try to avoid redundancy. What's more, litigation over the standard phrase *indemnify and hold harmless* (that's Romance and Saxon) gives pause. Some courts say the terms are synonyms, while others say they're not.[10] Ultimately, a knowledge of Saxon-Romance pairs might help you streamline and improve your contracts.

Plainness: Short forms, Initials, Acronyms, and Defined Names

Lawyers sometimes overuse initials, acronyms, and defined terms. Sometimes you can't avoid them, but often you can do better. Some advice:

If the seller in your agreement is Green Fish Marketing Company:

1. Don't use *hereinafter* phrases.

    No: Green Fish Marketing Company (hereinafter referred to as "Seller")

    Yes: Green Fish Marketing Company ("Seller")

2. Quotation marks are optional, but using them makes clear you're creating a shorthand name, not merely adding a parenthetical.

    Fine: Green Fish Marketing Company (Seller)

---

[9] *Id.* at 7.
[10] *Id.* at 292-93.

Also fine: Green Fish Marketing Company ("Seller")

3. Don't create a defined term and never use it.

   Lawyers create them out of habit and then never use them or create them and then end up deleting the later references—forgetting to delete the text creating the defined term.

4. Avoid alternatives—pick one.

   No: Green Fish Marketing Company ("Green Fish" or "Seller")

5. Default to what the party calls itself—don't invent initials.

   If the party calls itself "Green Fish," use that. If the party calls itself "GFMC," use that. But if the party calls itself "Green Fish," don't use "GFMC." (You'll need to be flexible if you have multiple parties with the same basic name: Green Fish Marketing Co., Green Fish Holding Co., Green Fish Management, etc.)

6. Prefer words to initials and acronyms when possible.

   Green Fish, not GFMC

7. Either consistently use or consistently omit *the*.

   Either "Seller agrees to ..." or "The Seller agrees to ..."

8. Descriptors (Seller) instead of names (Green Fish Marketing Company) are fine.

   Descriptors often make adapting a form easier, but be wary of *'or* and *'ee* correlates; they're easily confused and inadvertently swapped. So for *lessor/lessee* try *landlord/tenant*, for *grantor/grantee* try *seller/buyer*, and for *licensor/licensee* try *owner/licensee*.

✦✦✦

Not a Rule

Not a rule: You Must Use *Mr.*, *Ms.*, and So on

Some legal writers apply the titles *Mr.*, *Ms.*, and *Mrs.* to the people involved in a matter. These writers are being polite and professional.

But If your supervisor will allow it, you can drop *Mr.*, *Ms.*, and *Mrs.* So this:

> Mr. Yasar and Mr. Lira had worked at the fire department together for four years.

Becomes this:

> Yasar and Lira had worked at the fire department together for four years.

You've got Bryan Garner on your side if you do:

> Legal writers seem to fear looking impolite if they don't consistently use *Mr.*, *Ms.*, and so on. Actually, though, they're simply achieving a brisker, more matter-of-fact style. Journalists aren't being rude when they do this, and neither are you.[11]

You may also give the full name on first reference and shorten to surname without defining it. So this:

> Mr. Keith Cabler and Ms. Rory Askew have failed to state a valid claim against Gulf Coast, Inc., or its president, Ms. Myriam Puente. Mr. Cabler and Ms. Askew have also failed to effectuate proper service of process on Ms. Puente.

Becomes this:

---

[11] Bryan A. Garner, *The Winning Brief* 245 (3d ed. 2014).

> Keith Cabler ("Cabler") and Rory Askew ("Askew") have failed to state a valid claim against Gulf Coast, Inc., or its president, Myriam Puente ("Puente"). Cabler and Askew have also failed to effectuate proper service of process on Puente.

And then this:

> Keith Cabler and Rory Askew have failed to state a valid claim against Gulf Coast, Inc., or its president, Myriam Puente. Cabler and Askew have also failed to effectuate proper service of process on Puente.

And then use a pronoun (*they*) if it's not vague:

> Keith Cabler and Rory Askew have failed to state a valid claim against Gulf Coast, Inc., or its president, Myriam Puente. They also failed to properly serve process on Puente.

Not a Rule: Don't Begin with *However*

"My boss [professor, English teacher] told me never to begin a sentence with *however*."

I've heard this comment a number of times from law students and lawyers, and it's often followed with a sincere "Why?" I'll discuss where this advice comes from and suggest that it's a stylistic suggestion, not a rule.

The most likely source of this prohibition is *The Elements of Style* by Strunk and White. Their advice against beginning with *however* is consistent through four editions: "Avoid starting a sentence with *however* when the meaning is 'nevertheless.'"[12] Why that advice? Strunk and White believed that when *however* comes first, it means "in whatever way" or "to whatever extent."[13] Here's a pair of examples that show what they were thinking:

---

[12] William Strunk Jr. & E.B. White, *The Elements of Style* 48 (4th ed. 2000).
[13] *Id.* at 49.

a. However it turns out, the policy will cover the loss.

b. However, it turns out the policy will cover the loss.

In example a, *however* means "in whatever way," but in b it means "nevertheless." What distinguishes the meanings is the comma after *however* in example b. Apparently, Strunk and White worried that young writers (*The Elements of Style* is for college students, after all) would include or omit the comma incorrectly, creating an ambiguous *however*—hence the prohibition.

Under the prohibition, when you mean "nevertheless," you must move *however* into the sentence and set it off with commas. Here, examples c and d follow the rule against beginning with *however*, and example e breaks it.

c. The brief, however, does not address personal jurisdiction.

d. The brief does not, however, address personal jurisdiction.

e. However, the brief does not address personal jurisdiction.

Yet in reality, there's no rule against beginning with *however*. According to Bryan Garner, beginning with *however* is "not a grammatical error."[14] *Merriam Webster's Dictionary of English Usage* declares that "there is no absolute rule for the placement of *however*."[15] And Terri LeClercq says you may "use *however* in any position."[16]

So for the meaning "nevertheless" or "on the other hand," it's fine to begin with *however* [plus comma]. Legal writers can master comma rules sufficiently well to avoid the ambiguity Strunk and White feared. And beginning with *however* is not only grammatically justified, it has the advantage of signaling contrast for readers immediately, rather than later in the sentence. For example:

---

[14] Bryan A. Garner, *Garner's Dictionary of Legal Usage* 415 (3d ed. 2011).

[15] *Merriam Webster's Dictionary of English Usage* 515 (1994).

[16] Terri LeClercq, *Expert Legal Writing* 180 (1995).

g. We closed the deal on Thursday. However, the payment arrived on Friday.

Of course, you can also place *however* mid-sentence to create desired emphasis, as we saw in examples c and d above. If you use a pair of commas, make sure that *however* isn't separating independent clauses, which would require a semicolon and comma.

h. **Right:** We closed the deal on Thursday. The payment, however, arrived on Friday.

i. **Right:** We closed the deal on Thursday; however, the payment arrived on Friday.

j. **Wrong:** We closed the deal on Thursday, however, the payment arrived on Friday.

Example j is a run-on sentence or comma splice, an error I occasionally see in legal writing. Of course, you could use *but* in these sentences and simplify the punctuation while punching up the transition. In fact, if there's a stylistically justified reason to avoid beginning with *however*, it's that *however* is a heavy, multi-syllabic transition.

k. We closed the deal on Thursday, but the payment arrived on Friday.

l. We closed the deal on Thursday. But the payment arrived on Friday.

So if your boss or professor tells you not to begin with *however*, think of it as a stylistic suggestion—but one you're required to follow. Otherwise, place *however* where it creates the emphasis you want, even if that's at the beginning. And consider *but*.

Not a Rule: Don't Begin with *But*

Sure, it's a wise admonition from middle-school English teachers that novice writers avoid beginning a series of sentences with *but*. *We went to Six Flags. But it rained. But my mom said we could go later. But we didn't have time. But I really wanted to go.*

By high school, many English teachers embrace the beginning *but*. My son's 9th-grade English teacher includes "beginning with a conjunction" in a list of writing techniques, offering this example, *But how could this be?* and requiring students to create their own examples.

What? Teaching kids it's okay to begin a sentence with *but*? No wonder writing skills are in decline and college students (not to mention law students) don't write well. But wait. I applaud these high-school teachers, and they're in line with the general view of numerous writing authorities.

I refer you to Bryan Garner's article, *On Beginning Sentences with But*; *The Chicago Manual of Style* ("a perfectly proper word to open a sentence"); and the Internet, where a Google search for "beginning with but" turns up many reputable authorities recommending the practice.

As with many writing "rules," the truth is that beginning with *but* isn't about wrong or right; it's about formality, emphasis, and style. So don't uncritically apply this nonrule. Think about your writing goals and options and decide how you want to use the language.

Let's start with formality. Although we're probably already comfortable beginning with *but* in e-mail messages, print correspondence, and inter-office memos, some lawyers avoid the practice in formal documents like motions, briefs, and judicial opinions. Yet the technique has been used in formal legal documents for centuries. Here are some examples.

From a judicial opinion in 2013:

"But this case has nothing to do with federalism." *City of Arlington v. FCC*, 569 U.S. 290, 305 (2013).

From a judicial opinion in 1901:

"But this is not sufficient." *Colburn v. Grant*, 181 U.S. 601, 607 (1901).

From a judicial opinion in 1793:

"But this redress goes only half way." *Chisholm v. Georgia*, 2 U.S. 419, 422 (1793).

From an appellate brief in 2003:

"But the EPA cannot claim that ADEC's decision was unreasoned."
Alaska Dept. of Envtl. Conservation v. EPA, 2003 WL 2010655 at 46
(U.S. Pet. Brief 2003), quoted by Ross Guberman in *Point Made*.

And from the U.S. Constitution:

"But in all such Cases the Votes of both Houses shall be determined by
yeas and Nays." U.S. Const. art. I, § 7.

If we accept that beginning with *but* is appropriate for formal legal
documents, then it becomes a tool we can use to manage emphasis. Using
the example from *Arlington v. FCC*, note the differing emphases in these
three versions:

But this case has nothing to do with federalism.

- succinctly emphasizes the contrast

However, this case has nothing to do with federalism.

- contrasts but moves slowly

This case, however, has nothing to do with federalism.

- even slower and emphasizes *this case*

You can do more than use the technique for emphasis. Once you're
comfortable beginning with *but*, you can use it to create readable, crisp
transitions that quickly orient the reader to a change of direction. For
crisp transitions, *yet* is a great word to begin with, too.

From a judicial opinion in 1968:

"Yet we see no possible rational basis." *Glona v. Am. Guarantee &*
Liab. Ins. Co., 391 U.S. 73, 75 (1968).

Yes, you can begin with *however* or *in contrast* or *on the other hand*.
They're fine. But now we know that beginning with *but* is fine for formal
legal documents, gives us a tool for managing emphasis, and makes a

great connector. After all, there's no rule against beginning a sentence with *but*.

Not a Rule: Don't End with a Preposition

That's according to the Texas Law Review *Manual on Usage & Style*.

Is that authoritative? After all, the *MoUS* is written by students. Yet Bryan Garner agrees in *The Redbook*: the "rule" against ending a sentence with a preposition is "a superstition that just won't die." Strunk and White say so, too, in *The Elements of Style*: "Not only is the preposition acceptable at the end, sometimes it is more effective in that spot than anywhere else." Yes, that's the fourth edition from 2000, but the quoted language is unchanged from first Strunk & White edition in 1959.

Canvass the style manuals and writing references and websites—the answer is near universal. End a sentence with a preposition if you need to. Prepositions are perfectly good words to end sentences with. If you think there's a rule against ending with a preposition, you don't know what you're talking about.

So what's the deal?

First, a preliminary matter. I'm writing about writing, not speech, but ending with a preposition is fine in speech, right? That's something I hope we can agree on. In particular, we often end with prepositions when asking questions:

Who are you talking about?

Where did he disappear to?

What did you step on?

Most of us would never speak these stiff, over-formal versions:

About whom are you talking?

To where did he disappear?

On what did you step?

Back to writing. Despite the experts (the *MoUS*, Garner, Strunk & White), the supposed rule against ending propositions still causes lawyers to write sentences like this:

Attached are three local rules of which you should be aware.

A hammer, not an ax, was the weapon with which he struck the victim.

The deponent could not recall in which folder she saved the file.

These sentences are grammatically correct and have no ending prepositions, but to me they're stilted and unnatural. They don't flow.

One reason for these stilted sentences is that we know other lawyers believe the supposed rule, and we don't want to risk annoying those readers or, worse, seeming semi-literate. And so the circle spins on. We know it's okay to end with a preposition, but we also know some of our readers don't know it's okay, so we avoid doing it, perpetuating the no-ending-preposition practice.

What should we do? Rather than treat ending prepositions as wrong or right, a better approach is to think of them as a matter of formality and emphasis.

Ending with a preposition isn't wrong. It's less formal. That realization alone leads to some easy decisions. Appellate brief? A highly formal document for an audience whose grammar preferences you probably don't know well. Avoid ending with prepositions. Memo to a supervisor? A moderately formal document for an audience whose preferences you might know. Unless the audience objects, an occasional ending preposition is acceptable. Work e-mail to a colleague? An informal document to a well-known audience. Ending with prepositions is fine.

Ending with a preposition is also a matter of emphasis. You always have options, so you can always avoid ending with a preposition, but knowing when to do it requires experience and what we often call "a good ear." Here's an example.

Suppose you want to convey this idea:

Silver Partners refused to join any venture Hooper was part of.

That sentence strikes me as succinct and forceful. But you have other options that don't end with a preposition:

Silver Partners refused to join any venture if Hooper was part of it.

Or this:

If Hooper was part of the venture, Silver Partners refused to join.

But don't choose this option:

Silver Partners refused to join any venture of which Hooper was part.

It's often possible to avoid ending with a preposition, and avoiding has no risk. But I offer these two points. (1) Don't write the stilted, ending-preposition work-arounds like that last example (*of which Hooper was part*); they sound unnatural and affected. (2) If the preposition-ending sentence creates just the tone and emphasis you want, do it. After all, there is no rule against ending a sentence with preposition.

Note a Rule: Don't Split Infinitives

In English, the infinitive is a verb form constructed with *to* + the verb root, as in *to read*, *to write*, and *to edit*. The supposed rule against splitting an infinitive says you must not insert an adverb between *to* and the verb root; thus, these constructions break the rule: *to carefully read*, *to clearly write*, *to thoroughly edit*.

The no-split "rule" began as a misguided effort by early English grammarians to make English like Latin, in which the infinitive is a single word, like *scribere* (*to write*) and is therefore unsplit-able. If you can't split infinitives in Latin, they declared, then you mustn't in English.

But English isn't Latin. *Manifestum est.* In English, we have greater flexibility in placing adverbs to create desired tone and emphasis. So the "rule" is really a suggestion, and many experts say so:

"The principle of allowing split infinitives is broadly accepted as both normal and useful." —*Oxford A–Z Guide to English Usage*.

"It's fine to split infinitives. Certainly don't let anyone tell you it's for-
bidden." —Mignon Fogarty in *Grammar Girl's Quick and Dirty Tips for
Better Writing*.

"Split infinitives have long been an effective way to avoid awkward
writing." —Jan Venolia in *Write Right!*

"It is permissible to split an infinitive." —Joan Ames Magat in *The Lawyer's Editing Manual*.

"There is no 'rule' in English about split infinitives—just the common-
sense suggestion that adverbs should be placed where they sound
best." —Terri LeClercq in *Expert Legal Writing*.

Yet after consulting a dozen sources in preparing to write this section,
I will candidly report that the predominant advice is to avoid splitting
infinitives when you can. This means avoid splitting unless avoiding the
split is awkward. In other words—and this is my opinion—this non-rule
still has enough force that even experts who acknowledge there is no such
rule advise you to avoid splitting when you can.

My advice? Trust your ear and split the infinitive whenever splitting
sounds natural to you. Although legal writing can't always be modeled on
speech, this is one area where you should probably write it the way you
would say it.

For example, I gladly split the infinitive here: *He asked me to carefully
read the statute*, and I would never write this strained, split-infinitive
work-around: *He asked me carefully to read the statute*. (It's ambiguous,
too: what is careful, the asking or the reading?) But avoiding the split
would be simple and wouldn't result in awkwardness or loss of emphasis:
He asked me to read the statute carefully. That's a safe course if you think
your reader might be a no-splitter.

One more thing. Some writers take the non-rule against splitting infinitives and apply it to all verb phrases, which would mean you must not
insert an adverb between an auxiliary verb and the main verb. Applying
such a rule would mean verb phrases like *will execute*, *be convinced*, and

have demonstrated could not be split, like this: *will faithfully execute, be easily convinced*, and *have publicly demonstrated*. Based on my reading and research, those who believe in the rule against splitting verb phrases tend to be journalists or to have a journalism background.

Don't worry about splitting verb phrases. Besides the absence of a genuine rule, there's the awkwardness of the work-arounds, as in this example I recently read: *In recent weeks, two officials publicly have demonstrated distrust of Smith*. I hope you'll agree the split version is more natural: *In recent weeks, two officials have publicly demonstrated distrust of Smith*.

Ultimately, the split infinitive "has become a matter of minor concern," according to Tom MacArthur in *The Oxford Concise Companion to the English Language*. It ought to stay that way. If you trust your ear, you'll probably split more than not, and that's fine. After all, there's no rule against splitting an infinitive.

✦ ✦ ✦

Persuasion

Persuasion: Basic EMPHASIS!

How can legal writers create emphasis in the main text of an analytical document like a motion or brief? Here are some tips.

Typefaces emphasize. **Boldface**, *italics*, and ***bold italics*** will draw the reader's attention. But they almost work too well. They **stand out** from the main text so strongly they can become **distracting**. When readers read a bold italics word, they mentally **increase the volume** of the voice in their heads. Readers **literally emphasize** the emphasized text. That becomes **tiresome**. Tiresome emphasis irritates, and the intended emphasis **backfires**, annoying the reader. ***See what I mean?***

So use typefaces for emphasis sparingly.

Brevity emphasizes. Did you notice that in the midst of this section of normal-length paragraphs, the previous paragraph stands out? It's short—a single sentence. The contrast of a single-sentence paragraph with typical-length paragraphs creates emphasis. Notice also the first sentence in this paragraph: two words, subject and verb, direct and forceful. Brevity emphasizes. Yes, brevity can be overdone. Brevity becomes choppiness when you write lots of short sentences, so be wise.

Beginnings emphasize. Words and phrases that appear at the beginnings of paragraphs and sentences tend to draw emphasis. In particular, anyone or anything that appears as the subject of a sentence, or of several sentences, will be emphasized in readers' minds—a good reason to keep your subjects close to the beginnings of sentences.

Repetition emphasizes. A word or phrase that's repeated in your text will be emphasized in the reader's mind. As with any technique, of course, repeating key words can be overdone. But repetition means more than repeating key words; it means repeating structure, and that's called parallelism.

Parallelism emphasizes. Consider four types:

1. a simple list or series (the flag is red, white, and blue)

2. a complex series with identical grammatical structures

3. a large-scale parallel structure (the way the paragraphs in this section begin with _____ emphasize)

4. a numbered list (like the one you just read)

Endings emphasize. Just as the beginning of a sentence is a place of emphasis, each sentence has another place of emphasis—at the end. The last word of a sentence closes out a complete thought for the reader. It is therefore a good place to put a word you want to emphasize.

Dashes emphasize. If you have a concept you want to emphasize, consider setting it off with an em dash—like this. Or set it off with a pair of dashes—to create emphasis—like this. But don't overdo it—like this paragraph.

Ultimately, creating emphasis is important but challenging. **TOO MUCH CAN BACKFIRE!** So try these tips and pay attention to what you read. Seek to develop your sense of emphasis.

Persuasion: Research

A legal-writing teacher and a statistician studied intensifier use in Supreme Court briefs. Intensifiers are words that bolster, such as _very_, _clearly_, _obviously_, and the like. The authors state, correctly, that many experts on legal writing recommend against intensifiers and especially against overusing them. So they decided to measure intensifier use against outcomes—does using more intensifiers in a brief increase the likelihood of winning?

No.

Their research showed that using intensifiers frequently in a brief, particularly a brief for the appellant, is correlated with a greater likelihood of losing. The authors point out that they couldn't establish a causal connection—they couldn't prove it was the intensifiers that caused the briefs to lose—but the correlation is interesting.[17]

A second article, by the same authors, reports on a study of the readability of appellate briefs. The authors measured briefs according to the Flesch Reading Ease scale—a scale of zero to 100 that measures average word length and average sentence length. The higher the score, the more readable the text. (The briefs in the study tended to score in the low-to-mid 30s on the scale.) The authors measured readability scores against outcomes—does having a higher (better) readability score increase the likelihood of winning?

No.

Shorter sentences and smaller words won't necessarily win. The authors found no statistically significant relationship between a brief's readability score and its success.[18]

Is plainer writing more persuasive? What about informal writing? In a third article, the author, Sean Flammer, asked judges to decide which of two versions of a legal argument they considered more persuasive.

Half the judges chose between a traditional, legalese argument and a plainer version. The other half chose be-tween the legalese version and an informal version that used first person, contractions, and so on. The study collected responses from trial and appellate judges in state and federal courts and sorted the survey results by those criteria and by age, experience, sex, and geographical setting (rural or urban).

For the half of judges choosing between the legalese version and the plainer version, a majority preferred the plainer version:

---

[17] Lance N. Long & William F. Christensen, *Clearly, Using Intensifiers Is Very Bad—Or Is It?* 45 Idaho L. Rev. 171, 171 (2008).

[18] Lance N. Long & William F. Christensen, *Does the Readability of Your Brief Affect Your Chance of Winning an Appeal?—An Analysis of Readability in Appellate Briefs and Its Correlation with Success on Appeal,* 12 J. App. Prac. & Proc. 145 (2011).

Overall judge preference
for plain versus legalese

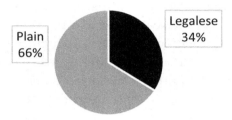

For the half choosing between the legalese version and the informal version, a smaller majority still preferred the informal to the legalese:

Overall judge preference
for informal versus legalese

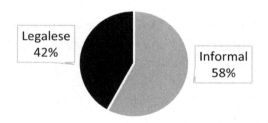

We don't yet have proof that better writing wins, but we can see that judges prefer plainer writing.[19]

---

[19] Sean Flammer, *Persuading Judges: An Empirical Analysis of Writing Style, Persuasion, and the Use of Plain English*, 16 Legal Writing 184 (2010).

Persuasion: Priming

Research and study are proving the cliché that first impressions matter. Specifically, we're learning that priming in a motion or brief can nudge the decision-maker.

Here's a definition of priming: "use of a stimulus, or prime, to alter audience members' perceptions of subsequent information."[20] Some priming is accidental, as seen in a study in Arizona: voters whose polling locations were inside schools were more likely to vote for increased school funding than those who voted elsewhere.[21]

Priming can be replicated in the lab. Professor Kathryn Stanchi of Temple Law described a study in which subjects (think "judges") had to decide whether a single mother would get an increase in government aid. First, the subjects were "primed" by having them read unrelated vignettes designed to elicit either anger or sadness. Later, when they had to decide the case, subjects primed for anger were less likely to increase aid; they tended to blame the mother for her situation. Subjects primed for sadness were more likely to increase aid; they tended to see her situation as caused by external factors.[22]

For persuasive legal writing, one priming technique would be writing a preliminary statement in a way that predisposes a reader to respond favorably to the later presentation of facts and law. In a recent study that assessed legal writing and judicial readers, Prof. Kenneth Chestek of Wyoming Law tested whether a negative preliminary statement or a positive one would affect judicial decision-making. His results showed that priming through a preliminary statement did affect judges' decisions—especially for the party perceived to be weaker.

---

[20] Michael J. Higdon, *Something Judicious This Way Comes … the Use of Foreshadowing As a Persuasive Device in Judicial Narrative*, 44 U. Rich. L. Rev. 1213, 1229 (2010).

[21] Daniel Kahneman, *Thinking, Fast and Slow* 58 (2011).

[22] Kathryn M. Stanchi, *The Power of Priming in Legal Advocacy: Using the Science of First Impressions to Persuade the Reader*, 89 Or. L. Rev. 305, 328 (2010).

In his study, Chestek recruited 163 real judges from all levels and from around the United States. The judges took a pre-survey questionnaire that would enable Chestek to control for pre-existing biases in his results. The judges then read an excerpt from a brief for summary judgment, pitting a small business against a federal agency. Each brief contained the same statement of facts and summary of the law, but they had nine different versions of the preliminary statement—four negative-themed, four positive-themed, and one neutral. Thus, the preliminary statement was the only thing that differed in the briefs.

Yet judges who read a preliminary statement that favored the small business tended to view the case more favorably to the small business than those who read the neutral preliminary statement. Judges who read a preliminary statement that favored a federal agency "were mixed, but were uniformly less favorable to the small business."[23] And, Chestek points out, given that the facts and the law were exactly the same, "all of this persuasion occurred in the Preliminary Statement: a brief glimpse at the theme that the brief writer has chosen for the rest of the brief."[24]

So priming can make a difference in persuasive legal writing: it can "help influence the decision maker's feel for the entire case."[25]

So how do you write a priming preliminary statement?

By "preliminary statement," I mean the opening substantive content of a motion, trial brief, administrative filing, or similar part of a similar document. It might be called an introduction or go by other names, but the point is that if the judge reads the document, the preliminary statement is the first substantive content.

To persuade and to prime, you must do more than recount the claim, defense, and procedural status. Yes, you need those contextual details

---

[23] Kenneth D. Chestek, *Fear and Loathing in Persuasive Writing: An Empirical Study of the Effects of the Negativity Bias*, 14 Legal Comm. & Rhetoric: JALWD 1, 28 (2017).

[24] *Id.*

[25] Stanchi, at 350.

because "the judge may not have read any other document in the case."[26] But don't stop there.

After supplying the context, it's time to prime. In his book *Point Made*, Ross Guberman asserts that one form of priming is to appeal to a judge's "fear of misconstruing a doctrine."[27] So if current law doesn't recognize a claim, the defending attorney should point that out in the preliminary statement. (In all the examples, procedural context is omitted.) For example:

> Marin cannot proceed with a *Sabine Pilot* claim because the Texas Supreme Court has not recognized a constructive-discharge theory under the *Sabine Pilot* doctrine. What's more, Marin gave reasons for his resignation that are unrelated to any request to commit an illegal act; thus, he cannot fulfill *Sabine Pilot*'s "sole cause" requirement.

Another type of priming is an appeal to fairness. As Guberman puts it, you aim to appeal to the decision-maker's "fear of reaching an unfair result or causing harm."[28] Judges want to do the right thing, he says, so effective writers go "beyond the case law and the record, giving the judge a pragmatic reason to want to rule for them."[29]

For example, in an SEC proceeding in which the government withheld a document from the defendant without describing it, the defense lawyer recounted the procedural background and then asserted that his client should not

> be forced to make crucial decisions—such as whether to invoke his Fifth Amendment privilege—with his eyes closed and his hands tied. This would be both unfair and unconstitutional.[30]

---

[26] Kamela Bridges & Wayne Schiess, *Writing for Litigation* (2d ed. 2020).
[27] Ross Guberman, *Point Made* 28 (2d ed. 2014).
[28] *Id*. at 32.
[29] *Id*. at 38.
[30] *Id*. at 33.

This is an overt appeal to both fairness and law, priming the reader to be sympathetic to the defendant.

You might also try to offer a compelling narrative—tell a story.[31] Here's an example (procedural context omitted):

> Dani Wilcox suffered a broken jaw and cheekbone when one of the Defendant officers kicked her in the head in the course of an arrest on March 4, 2010. Wilcox's injuries required insertion of two metal plates and eight screws into her jawbone. The beating also left her with a permanent loss of sensation.[32]

Note that the date is present but isn't used as an opener.

And if sympathy and narrative aren't available, an appeal to the rule of law can be a form of priming:

> Although, as Applicant has noted, one of the two arrests resulted in no charge, the other resulted in conviction, precluding Applicant's licensure. Despite the recommendation letters and Applicant's expressions of remorse, the Hearing Officer has no discretion, under ADM § 9.01(1)(b), to approve licensure for an applicant whose conviction occurred within the preceding five years.

Give it a try. By adding a form of priming to the preliminary statement in addition to the procedural context, you invite the decision-maker to engage with the dispute in a way that favors your client and increases your chances of prevailing.

Persuasion: Up-Front Summaries

Every legal document longer than a page or two should begin with a summary of some kind, but you don't have to take my word for it.

---

[31] Amy Bitterman, *In the Beginning: The Art of Crafting Preliminary Statements*, 45 Seton Hall L. Rev. 1009, 1019 (2015).

[32] *Id.* at 1024-25.

"All legal writing should be front loaded. It should start with a capsule version of the analysis. It should practice the art of summarizing."[33]

"By establishing the main points of a document before launching into a detailed analysis of the points, you show readers what information to look for."[34]

"Why is it important for legal writers to lead with their conclusions? There are three main reasons: It's more convincing. It's easier to read for the first time. And a hasty or dimwitted reader can still understand it."[35]

"All briefs should have a first-page, introductory summary whether the rules require one or not."[36]

"One of my partners says he begins the preliminary statement as if he had 30 seconds on the evening news to pitch his case. He shapes his opening like the lead sentence in a news article-focused and factual."[37]

"In each part of your legal analysis, give the bottom line first, plainly and without fanfare."[38]

"[Regarding *COMES NOW*,] by devoting the entire opening paragraph to restating the needlessly long title, lawyers waste judges' time and sacrifice a valuable chance for persuasion."[39]

---

[33] Joseph Kimble, *Lifting the Fog of Legalese* 73 (2007).
[34] Frederic G. Gale & Joseph M. Moxley, *How to Write the Winning Brief* 107 (1992).
[35] Steven D. Stark, *Writing to Win: The Legal Writer* 144 (1999).
[36] *Id.* at 8-10.
[37] Kenneth Oettle, *Making Your Point* 85 (2007).
[38] Irwin Alterman, *Plain and Accurate Style in Court Papers* 97 (1987).
[39] Beverly Ray Burlingame, *On Beginning a Court Paper*, 6 Scribes J. Leg. Writing 160, 161 (1996-1997).

"By providing an overview of the document's content before the main body of the text, you make it easier for the user to read and understand the whole document."[40]

"A summary gives the big picture—the main points of a document. When readers see the main points first, they can more easily absorb the detailed information that supports them."[41]

"I have run across those who thought this was the way to write reports: Feed out details gradually, "create suspense," save the big news to the last. But this is a poor way to organize a piece of writing that is chiefly information."[42]

"Knowing where a discussion or argument is heading is essential if a reader is to understand on first reading."[43]

"I know of only one good reason for saving big news till the end—deliberate obfuscation."[44]

"All legal writing should begin with an up-front summary of the important information, whether a preview, a thesis, or a mini-outline."[45]

Get it?

Yes, it's natural to want to give the background first—before the point, before the argument, before the question. But legal readers are eager to know what you want to say or what you want to get—and why.

Don't worry about previewing the whole document in the summary and then repeating yourself in the body. Be concise with your summary

---

[40] Daniel B. Felker et al., *Guidelines for Document Designers* 13 (1981).
[41] Robert Dubose, *Legal Writing for the Rewired Brain* 87 (2010).
[42] Robert Gunning, *The Technique of Clear Writing* 130 (1968).
[43] Lynn B. Squires, Marjorie Dick Rombauer & Katherine See Kennedy, *Legal Writing in a Nutshell* 32-33 (2d ed. 1996).
[44] Martin Cutts, *Oxford Guide to Plain English* 134 (2004).
[45] Wayne Schiess, *Plain Legal Writing: Do It* 59 (2019).

and remember—summaries don't always need a lot of detail. It might be enough to preview what and how much is coming.

Don't worry that readers will read the summary and skip the rest. All readers do it; you do it, too. So rather than pretending that you can force readers to read the whole thing, admit that many will just skip to the end if you don't summarize up front.

One note on up-front summaries: even though the summary appears first in the document, you usually can't write it first. You should do at least one draft of the entire document. Then you'll know what belongs in the summary.

Persuasion: Quoting

Legal writers often need to use quotations in persuasive documents. Quoting a reliable source adds credibility to your assertions and can relieve the reader of independently checking a source. In this section I'll discuss a technique for formally introducing quotations that can enhance persuasive force and invite readers to read the quotation—not skip it.

But first, two caveats: (1) Legal writing requires scrupulous honesty and care in quoting; misquoting a source, intentionally or accidently, harms your credibility. (2) Legal writers should avoid over-quoting; use quotations for crucial legal language or to clinch a key point. Otherwise, paraphrase.

Finally, I'm not talking about incorporating a quotation into your own textual sentence, like these examples:

The relevant statute states, "any taxpayer who paid the sales tax has standing to sue for a refund." [citation]

The relevant statute provides that "any taxpayer who paid the sales tax has standing to sue for a refund." [citation]

Instead, I'll address a formal lead-in to a quotation.

A common and traditional way to introduce a quotation is to use a lead-in statement and a colon, like these:

The court stated as follows:

The statute provides the following:

The hearing officer made the following ruling:

These forms are adequate but average. In their place, I recommend introducing the quotation with what we might call an informative or persuasive lead-in by asserting a point the quotation will prove.

So don't write this:

> The relevant statute provides authorization as follows: "Any taxpayer who paid the sales tax has standing to sue for a refund." [citation]

Instead, introduce the quotation by asserting a point the quotation will clinch, like this:

> The Tax Code affirms Granger's right to sue for a refund: "Any taxpayer who paid the sales tax has standing to sue for a refund." [citation]

The technique works for block quotations, too. We all know that readers often skip block quotations. According to Mark Hermann, author of *The Curmudgeon's Guide to Practicing Law*, "you must trick the judge into learning the content of the block quotation."[46] He recommends summarizing the quotation's substance in the lead-in sentence. And Bryan Garner, in *The Winning Brief*, offers similar advice: "For every block quotation, supply an informative, eye-catching lead-in."[47]

So instead of this average lead-in:

> The State intervened in operating Lincoln County Schools, and the Superintendent thus acted under authority of the Education Code, which states as follows:

> > The state board shall intervene in the operation of a school district to cause improvements to be made that will provide

---

[46] Mark Herrmann, *The Curmudgeon's Guide to Practicing Law* 8 (2006).
[47] Bryan A. Garner, *The Winning Brief* 501 (3d ed. 2014).

> assurances of a thorough and efficient system of schools. Such in-
> tervention includes the authority of the state superintendent to
> fill positions of administrators and principals.

[citation]

Try this:

> Once the State intervened in operating Lincoln County Schools, the Ed-
> ucation Code granted the Superintendent the right to make personnel
> decisions for the vacant principal positions:
>
> > The state board shall intervene in the operation of a school dis-
> > trict to cause improvements to be made that will provide assur-
> > ances of a thorough and efficient system of schools. Such inter-
> > vention includes the authority of the state superintendent to fill
> > positions of administrators and principals.

[citation]

The lead-in asserts a point and, to some degree, summarizes the quotation to follow. With this technique, according to Herrmann and Garner,
you'll get two payoffs. First, readers might read the block: the assertive
tone of the lead-in invite them to read the quotation to see if you're right.
Second, even if readers skip the block, they still get the content.

Persuasion: Block Quotations

A survey of the advice on block quotations shows that it's almost all negative: Don't do it unless you must, say judges, legal-writing teachers, and
experienced lawyers. So we should block block quotations? Why? Two
main reasons.

Readers skip them. These readers include judges and their clerks. Admit it—you often skip block quotations when you read, too, so why would
your readers be any different? If you put something important in a block
quotation, you risk that it won't be read.

They smack of laziness. Instead of paraphrasing, instead of summarizing, you used a block quotation—you copied and pasted. That's the impression block quotations give, especially if you overuse them, and that perceived laziness turns readers off.

Despite these concerns, many well-written memos and briefs contain at least one block quotation and sometimes more. So the point is not to ban block quotations but to use them sparingly and effectively. Here are some recommendations.

First, anything you block-quote must be vital. If statutory language is at issue or is crucial to your analysis, a block quotation is appropriate. And sometimes, block-quoting key statutory text can allow readers to get re-anchored in the relevant language by flipping or scrolling back to it without having to consult an appendix. Likewise, if a binding case contains language of more than 50 words that is directly relevant to your argument or powerfully persuasive for your position, a block quotation is appropriate. But if you harbor doubts about how vital the quotation is, you probably shouldn't use a block quotation.

Even after you decide you need that quotation, try to shorten it to fewer than 50 words—just so you can avoid a block quotation. Yes, an embedded quotation of 49 words is still off-putting, but it's more likely to be read because it isn't a block.

Now, if the text is 50 words or longer and you're certain you need it, edit it again so that when block-quoted, it's not too long. No page-length block quotations, please. One thing more annoying than a block quotation is a long block quotation.

As you edit, show your alterations and omissions per *Bluebook* rules, but remember: heavy alteration or omission suggests that the quotation might be taken out of context, so go easy. One lawyer recommends that if you've heavily edited the block quotation, drop a footnote that contains the full text so readers can check your work.[48]

As a last step, write an inviting, persuasive lead-in to the block. The lead-in needs to show why the quotation is important or assert something the quotation will prove. In fact, it's acceptable to paraphrase the quotation's key point and use that paraphrase as a lead-in. Think of it like this: The lead-in should make the reader think, "Hmm. Is that so? Well maybe I should read this block quotation to be sure." A colleague suggested to me that the text *after* the block quotation might assert the key point, too. Readers who skip the block will still get the point—twice.

Finally, are you going to strictly follow *The Bluebook*'s rule on length? In rule 5.2, *The Bluebook* says you must block only quotations of 50 words or more. But I say you can treat that rule as a recommendation, not binding authority. If you have a shorter quotation you'd like to highlight, you may set it off as a block if you wish.

Ultimately, you're in charge of your block quotations, so use them sparingly but effectively.

Persuasion: Subordination

Subordination uses a dependent clause that begins with a *subordinating adverb*; it "subordinates" the dependent clause to the main clause. Subordinating adverbs, also called *subordinating conjunctions*, often involve time:

> after, before, since, until, when, whenever, while

They can also involve causation and other relationships:

> although, as, because, despite, if, though, unless, whereas, whether

> Subordination can occur before or after the main clause:

---

[48] Maureen Johnson, *To Quote or Not to Quote: Making the Case for Teaching Law Students the Art of Effective Quotation in Legal Memoranda*, 56 S. Tex. L. Rev. 283, 306 (2014).

Opening subordination

Although Arian's U.S. citizen children would suffer hardship if they moved to Ecuador, he has not shown the required exceptional and extremely unusual hardship.

Concluding subordination

Arian has not shown the required exceptional and extremely unusual hardship, although his U.S. citizen children would suffer hardship if they moved to Ecuador.

When an introductory, subordinated clause gets long, it inhibits easy reading:

Although Arian's U.S. citizen children, Olivia and Pirra, would suffer hardship—given that they are enrolled in school in Houston—if they were suddenly required to uproot themselves and make a family move to Ecuador, Arian has not shown the required exceptional and extremely unusual hardship.

Subordination for emphasis

Legal writers can use subordination to manage emphasis. The best technique is to—

- Place the idea to be de-emphasized in an opening, subordinated clause.
- Place the idea to be emphasized in a concluding, main clause.

So if you want to emphasize Arian's failure to make the required showing, you write this:

Although Arian's U.S. citizen children would suffer hardship if they moved to Ecuador, he has not shown the required exceptional and extremely unusual hardship.

This construction creates a subtle but "triple" emphasis:

- Readers give reduced emphasis to subordinated clauses.
- Readers give mental emphasis to main clauses.

- Readers give mental emphasis to concluding words—the last impression.

Persuasion: Are You Blatantly Bolstering?

As legal writers, we might be tempted to use intensifiers to bolster our points—to persuade. What's an intensifier? It's a linguistic element used to give emphasis or additional strength to another word or statement. Intensifiers can be various parts of speech: adverbs (*clearly*), adjectives (*blatant*), participles (*raving*), and more.

Intensifiers get a lot of bad press, and *clearly* is king:

Clearly is so overused in legal writing that one has to wonder if it has any meaning left. —Enquist & Oates in *Just Writing*

Doctrinaire adverbs such as *clearly* and *obviously* are perceived as signaling overcompensation for a weak argument. —Bryan A. Garner in *The Winning Brief*

When most readers read a sentence that begins with something like *obviously*, *undoubtedly*, and so on, they reflexively think the opposite. —Joseph M. Williams in *Style: Lessons in Clarity and Grace*

One article on intensifiers in legal writing suggests that overusing intensifiers is bad—or *very bad*. In *Clearly, Using Intensifiers is Very Bad—Or Is It?*, their study of U.S. Supreme Court briefs, Lance Long and William Christensen found that increased intensifier use was correlated with losing, especially for appellants. The authors allege no causal connection—they couldn't prove it was the intensifiers that lost the case—but the correlation is interesting.

What can we do instead of overusing intensifiers? Three suggestions.

Drop them.

Often, a sentence gets stronger without the intensifier. Which of these is more forceful?

1. Clearly, an attorney is not an expert on what is a "Doberman," and there is no showing in the affidavit that Squires is an expert on Dobermans. It clearly is a fact issue for the trier of fact.

1a. An attorney is not an expert on what is a "Doberman," and there is no showing in the affidavit that Squires is an expert on Dobermans. It is a fact issue for the trier of fact.

Dropping intensifiers doesn't always work, and we can't completely banish them. Some legal standards require them: clearly erroneous, highly offensive. Legal writing entails some qualifying, but good legal writers develop a sense for when they're appropriately qualifying and when they're blatantly bolstering.

Replace them.
With some thought, you can delete an intensifier-plus-verb or intensifier-plus-noun construction and replace it with a single, forceful word. So—

This ...	*becomes this:*
completely wrong	inaccurate, incorrect, mistaken
extremely smart	brilliant
highly capable	accomplished, proficient
quickly went	hustled, sped, rushed
very sure	certain

Again, develop an editorial sense. Replacements don't always work; sometimes a single-word option is loaded. If instead of "very bad" you write "terrible" or "dreadful," you might interject undesired subjectivity or emotion.

Specify.
Rather than rely on a vague intensifier, legal writers can use details to emphasize. Here's a classic example:

2. It was very hot.

2a. It was 103 degrees in the shade.

Here's another example of specifying, with two more persuasion techniques: a dash and a sentence that ends with key words:

3. The transaction at issue obviously did not take place at Eason's residence.

3a. Lubbock detectives set up a controlled purchase with a cooperating defendant at Jay's Auto Body. It was there that Eason handed over a bag of methamphetamine—not at Eason's residence.

As you can see, specifying takes more words, and so, as with all writing, exercise editorial judgment. Weigh the longer, specific description against the shorter, vaguer (and weaker) one.

Persuasion: The Saxon Finish and the Saxon Restatement

Here we discuss two techniques for creating memorable, persuasive prose, which I discovered in Ward Farnsworth's forthcoming book, *Classical English Style*. By the way, how're you doing at spotting Saxon and Romance words? Try this: name the Saxon alternative for each Romance verb: *cogitate, emancipate, imbibe, inundate, masticate.*

In persuasive writing, some judges prefer Saxon words: "The best advocates will master the short Saxon word that pierces the mind like a spear." Hon. Robert H. Jackson, U.S. Supreme Court.[49] Another example: "A healthy respect for the robust Anglo-Saxon appeals more than does the Latin." Hon. Wiley B. Rutledge, U.S. Supreme Court.[50]

We can take advantage of this preference with two persuasive-writing techniques that combine Saxon words with Romance words—relying on

---

[49] Collected in Bryan A. Garner, *Judges on Effective Writing: The Importance of Plain Language*, Mich. B.J. 44-45 (Feb. 2005).
[50] *Id.*

differences in tone, formality, and force. The two techniques are the Saxon Restatement and the Saxon Finish.

The Saxon Restatement

With this technique, you state a proposition using primarily Romance words and then restate it using primarily Saxon words (or vice versa). Abraham Lincoln did it in his House Divided speech:

> "I do not expect the Union to be dissolved; I do not expect the house to fall."[51]

Lincoln essentially says the same thing twice: with Romance words (*union*, *dissolve*) and then Saxon (*house*, *fall*). He names lofty concepts and then brings them down to earth, creating a forceful, memorable couplet.

Winston Churchill did something similar in a famous speech:

> "I have nothing to offer but blood, toil, tears, and sweat. We have before us an ordeal of the most grievous kind."[52]

Here Churchill reversed the pattern, starting with Saxon (*blood*, *toil*, *tears*, and *sweat*) and reiterating with Romance (*ordeal* and *grievous*). The real, physical sacrifices are named and then connected to the abstract concepts.

I've created examples by modifying text from appellate briefs:

> The jury justifiably relied on the photographic evidence because images are unable to prevaricate; pictures cannot lie.

Here, *image*, *able*, and *prevaricate* are Romance; *cannot* and *lie* are Saxon. The lofty legal concepts are made concrete. Another example:

> Albrecht's only obligation under the order was to remunerate the seller for the vehicle she purchased—to pay for what she bought.

---

[51] Quoted in Ward Farnsworth, *Classical English Style* (forthcoming).
[52] *Id.*

The Saxon Finish

With this technique, you state a single proposition, but after beginning with Romance words, you finish with Saxon. Oliver Wendell Holmes did it well. Here are two examples from his dissenting opinions—the Saxon Finish is italicized:

> "If in the long run the beliefs expressed in proletarian dictatorship are destined to be accepted by the dominant forces of the community, the only meaning of free speech is that they should be *given their chance and have their way.*"[53]

> "If there is any principle of the Constitution that more imperatively calls for attachment than any other it is the principle of free thought—not free thought for those who agree with us but *freedom for the thought that we hate.*"[54]

Holmes builds up to a big idea with Romance words; then he states the idea with Saxon words. The result is a forceful wrap-up. I'll give it a try:

> Grayco asks this court to affirm the trial court's interpretation of section 216(b) so that punitive damages are grafted onto the text—an interpretation that produces an entirely different class of remedy from mere legislative silence. Grayco asks too much.

> The drug would be located in the deceased's system only under illicit conditions because having the drug is against the law.

Granted, these techniques are used most often in speech. Still, you should add them to your toolkit for persuasive legal writing. They constitute sophisticated rhetorical devices—they're tools of plain English.

---

[53] *Gitlow v. New York*, 268 U.S. 652, 673 (1925) (Holmes, J., dissenting).
[54] *United States v. Schwimmer*, 279 U.S. 644, 655 (1929) (Holmes, J., dissenting).

Persuasion: Qualifying Facts

Legal writing deals with concepts that often require qualification, so legal writers occasionally use qualifiers. (I used two in that sentence: *often* and *occasionally*.) In this section I define qualifiers and discuss the experts' advice for using them when writing about facts. I then offer two recommendations.

A qualifier is a word or phrase, especially an adverb or adjective, that clarifies or modifies another word. We use qualifiers to soften or limit, and intensifiers to strengthen and bolster. It's the difference between "the cleaning solution was *somewhat* defective" (qualifier) and "the cleaning solution was *highly* defective" (intensifier).

The most common fact qualifiers in legal writing relate to frequency and quantity. Here's a representative list:

generally	often
occasionally	probably
usually	slightly
sometimes	somewhat
typically	virtually

Advice from the experts is uniform: qualifiers applied to factual statements are undesirable in legal writing. In fact, *Garner's Dictionary of Legal Usage* contains an entry on qualifiers called Weasel Words, and Garner says these words "have the effect of rendering uncertain or toothless the statements in which they appear."[55] New York trial judge Gerald Lebovits says that instead of using words like *typically* or *usually*, legal writers should "resort to the exact figure or rethink your decision to resort to the qualifier in the first place."[56]

---

[55] Bryan A. Garner, *Garner's Dictionary of Legal Usage* 938 (3d ed. 2011).
[56] Gerald Lebovits, *The Worst Mistakes in Legal Writing, Part 4*, N.Y. State B. Assoc. J. 60, 63 (June 2018).

Steven Stark, a trial lawyer and the author of *Writing to Win*, says, "Opinions can be qualified, but facts should not be."[57] He advises, "If you don't know a fact, don't hedge—find it out or somehow write around it."[58] And one of my colleagues, also an experienced trial lawyer, "views a qualifier as a red flag—either the attorney hasn't nailed this fact down yet or it may not be true."

That's all good advice, and I'll add only one comment. You can't eliminate all qualifiers. They're occasionally (qualifier) necessary, and sometimes (qualifier) harmless. For example, there's no flaw in this sentence: "About half the time, Crosby, not the supervisor, gave the instructions." The qualifier (*about*) serves only to soften the possible implication that the half was exact—precisely 50%. That's harmless.

So rather than banishing qualifiers, the better practice (as with all legal-writing tips) is to inform yourself of their effects and exercise your editorial judgment as to keeping or cutting.

Now the tips.

1. Drop the qualifier.

Your fact statement might be better without the qualifier, and it'll certainly be more concise. So instead of "the cleaning solution was somewhat defective," you can write, "the cleaning solution was defective."

Here's another example: "The average person usually waits three months before seeing a doctor." The idea is already qualified by the "average person," so we can omit *usually*: "The average person waits three months before seeing a doctor."

2. Quantify or specify instead.

Another tip is to replace the qualifier with specifics. For example, here the writer uses *virtually* to make a general statement: "There is virtually no seismic data on the Freda Turk Ranch." If there's no data, we can apply

---

[57] Steven D. Stark, *Writing to Win: The Legal Writer* 45 (2d ed. 2012).
[58] *Id.* at 46.

tip number 1 and write, "There is no seismic data on the Freda Turk Ranch." But if there's some data, it's better to specify: "There were two seismic surveys completed 22 years ago on only a portion of the Freda Turk Ranch."

Persuasion: Qualifying Law

Legal matters are often qualified: some conclusions might merit *absolutely* and *certainly*, while others deserve *possibly* and *likely*. So legal writers justifiably use qualifiers.

Relying on a survey of legal-writing textbooks, I can report commonly recommended qualifiers for legal conclusions: *likely, probably, plausibly, possibly,* and *should.*

The most frequently recommended are *likely* and its forms, with *probably* coming in second. Many of the textbooks surveyed discuss the traditional, predictive memorandum, in which a lawyer predicts an outcome that may be less than certain. But these words are useful in other contexts, too—whenever a lawyer gives advice or offers a recommendation.

Likely and its forms are part of a useful continuum from positive to negative certainty. At one end is a direct *yes* or *will*—a legal result will happen; the outcome is certain. At the other is *no* or *will not*. In between are *likely* and *unlikely*, which might be further qualified: *highly likely, highly unlikely,* and so on.

Now the advice.

1. Don't qualify.

As with much writing advice for adverbs, adjectives, intensifiers, and qualifiers, the best advice is to avoid them when you can. Bryan Garner recommends that legal writers "toss out timid phrases."[59] What's more, he calls these qualifiers Fudge Words and offers as an undesirable

---

[59] Bryan A. Garner, *The Elements of Legal Style* 35 (2d ed. 2002).

example, "It would seem to appear that ...."[60] That's a trifecta: three Fudge Words in one clause: *would*, *seem*, and *appear*.

The urge to qualify is natural, but legal writers must be careful of "overhedging." Granted that legal outcomes are rarely certain, we sometimes overcorrect and qualify too much. It's a natural tendency, and novices might be particularly vulnerable.

In fact, a colleague in another state forbids his first-year students to qualify conclusions at all. He believes it forces them to research carefully, analyze precisely, and write clearly.[61] But even if you don't enforce a prohibition, it's a good default: don't qualify. For example:

Before

> A **possible** lawsuit by Heather Green against her employer, Manzares
> & Cline LLP, **likely could not** survive a motion to dismiss.

After

> Heather Green's suit against her employer, Manzares & Cline LLP,
> would not survive a motion to dismiss.

2. Qualify and explain.

When you decide that you must qualify your conclusion, that you must hedge, do your best to explain why—immediately and concretely. Explaining has two benefits.

You benefit. Forcing yourself to articulate why you've qualified your conclusion can lead to insights about the level of qualification. Maybe you over- or under-qualified your conclusion, which you can see now that you've had to explain it. Revise accordingly.

---

[60] Bryan A. Garner, *Garner's Dictionary of Legal Usage* 381 (3d ed. 2011).
[61] Andrew J. Turner, *Helping Students Grow Professionally and Overcome Fear: The Benefits of Teaching Unqualified Brief Answers*, 25 Perspectives: Teaching Legal Res. & Writing 3, 4-5 (2016).

Readers benefit. Explaining why you qualified a conclusion serves clients and decision-makers. They already know that *likely* means better than 50-50 but not a sure thing. By explaining, you empower them to ask additional questions or pursue other options.

Here's an example:

> Heather Green's suit against her employer, Manzares & Cline LLP, **likely would not** survive a motion to dismiss. Generally, employees may sue for retaliatory discharge because it encourages them to report illegal activity. But in-house-counsel employees may not sue because attorneys already have an incentive—an ethical obligation—to disclose illegal activity. Green was not in-house but was a law-firm associate and had no attorney-client relationship with her employer. Yet she was under the same ethical obligation to disclose illegal activity.

So set your default at no qualifications, but when you must qualify, be clear about why.

✦ ✦ ✦

The Best Sources on Legal Writing

Legal-writing references

- Bryan A. Garner, *Garner's Dictionary of Legal Usage* (3d ed. 2011).
- Bryan A. Garner, *The Redbook: A Manual on Legal Style* (4th ed. 2018).
- Texas Law Review, *Manual on Usage & Style* (14th ed. 2017).
- Anne Enquist & Laurel Currie Oates, *Just Writing: Grammar, Punctuation, and Style for the Legal Writer* (4th ed. 2013).
- Deborah Bouchoux, *Aspen Handbook for Legal Writers* (4th ed. 2017).
- Joan Ames Magat, *The Lawyer's Editing Manual* (2008).

English references

- *The Chicago Manual of Style* (17th ed. 2017).
- Bryan A. Garner, *Garner's Modern American Usage* (4th ed. 2016).
- June Casagrande, *The Best Punctuation Book, Period* (2014).

General legal writing

- Tom Goldstein & Jethro K. Lieberman, *The Lawyer's Guide to Writing Well* (3d ed. 2016).
- Bryan A. Garner, *Legal Writing in Plain English: A Text with Exercises* (2d ed. 2013).
- Bryan A. Garner, *The Elements of Legal Style* (2d ed. 2002).
- Joseph Kimble, *Lifting the Fog of Legalese* (2006).
- Wayne Schiess, *Legal Writing Nerd: Be One* (2018)

General writing

- Mignon Fogarty, *Grammar Girl's Quick and Dirty Tips for Better Writing* (2008).

- Patricia T. O'Conner, *Woe is I: The Grammarphobe's Guide to Better English in Plain English* (3d ed. 2010).
- William Zinsser, *On Writing Well* (6th ed. 2001).
- John R. Trimble, *Writing with Style: Conversations on the Art of Writing* (3d ed. 2010).
- Joseph M. Williams & Gregory G. Colomb, *Style: The Basics of Clarity and Grace* (4th ed. 2010).

General legal writing and legal language
- Adam Freedman, *The Party of the First Part: The Curious World of Legalese* (2007).
- David Mellinkoff, *The Language of the Law* (1963).
- Peter M. Tiersma, *Legal Language* (1999).

Brief-writing, persuasion, litigation writing
- Bryan A. Garner, *The Winning Brief: 100 Tips for Persuasive Briefing in Trial and Appellate Courts* (3d ed. 2014).
- Antonin Scalia & Bryan A. Garner, *Making Your Case: The Art of Persuading Judges* (2008).
- Kamela Bridges & Wayne Schiess, *Writing for Litigation* (2d ed. 2020).
- Ross Guberman, *Point Made: How to Write Like the Nation's Top Advocates* (2d ed. 2014).
- Michael R. Smith, *Advanced Legal Writing: Theories and Strategies in Persuasive Writing* (3d ed. 2012).

Legal drafting
- Kenneth A. Adams, *A Manual of Style for Contract Drafting* (4th ed. 2018).
- Tina Stark (ed.), *Negotiating and Drafting Contract Boilerplate* (2002).
- Tina Stark, *Drafting Contracts: How and Why Lawyers Do What They Do* (2d ed. 2013).

- Bryan A. Garner, *Garner's Guidelines for Drafting and Editing Contracts* (2019).

Plain English

- Rudolf Flesch, *How to Write Plain English*: *A Book for Lawyers and Consumers* (1979).
- Joseph Kimble, *Writing for Dollars, Writing to Please* (2012).
- Joseph Kimble, *Seeing Through Legalese: More Essays on Plain Language* (2017)
- Wayne Schiess, *Plain Legal Writing: Do It* (2019).

Document design

- Matthew Butterick, *Typography for Lawyers: Essential Tools for Polished and Persuasive Documents* (2d ed. 2018).
- Robert DuBose, *Legal Writing for the Rewired Brain: Persuading Readers in a Paperless World* (2010).
- Robin Williams, *The PC Is Not a Typewriter* (1995); *The Mac Is Not a Typewriter* (2d ed. 2003).

Practicing law

- Mark Herrmann, *The Curmudgeon's Guide to Practicing Law* (2006).
- Morten Lund, *Jagged Rocks of Wisdom—The Legal Memo: Mastering the Legal Memorandum* (2009).

Academic legal writing

- Eugene Volokh, *Academic Legal Writing: Law Review Articles, Student Notes, Seminar Papers, and Getting on Law Review* (4th ed. 2010).
- Elizabeth Fajans & Mary R. Falk, *Scholarly Writing for Law Students: Seminar Papers, Law Review Notes and Law Review Competition Papers* (3d ed. 2005).
- Jessica Lynn Wherry & Kristen E. Murray, *Scholarly Writing: Ideas, Examples, and Execution* (3d ed. 2019).

Made in the USA
Middletown, DE
25 August 2019